# CONTENTS

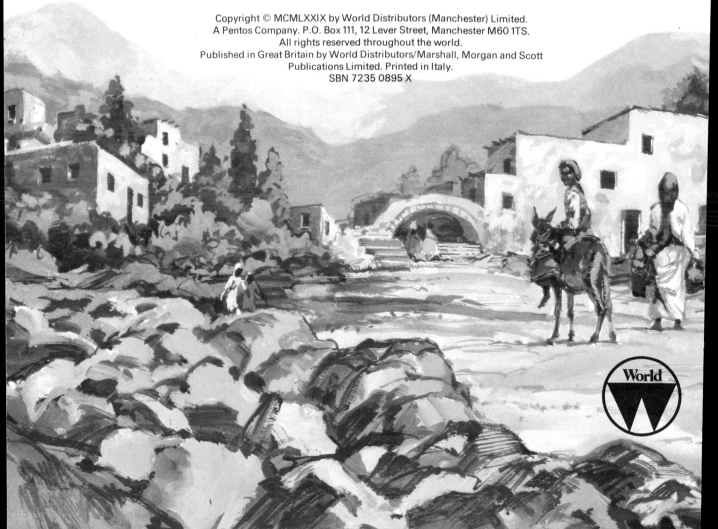

# THE BIBLE BOOK

## OLD and NEW TESTAMENT

Written by Katherine McLean

Illustrated by Edgar Hodges

# FOREWORD

The Bible has been called 'the greatest book in the world'.
It certainly is, for its stories are more stirring and
dramatic than any tale ever conceived by a storyteller.

This book contains such stories. But as well as stories
it also presents fascinating background information
about the people of the Bible, the lands they lived in,
their customs and history. I hope you enjoy reading
this book as much as I have enjoyed delving into all
sorts of reference books to gather these facts together,
to bring the Bible and its people vividly to life for you.

# IN THE BEGINNING

The Hebrews called the Book in the Bible which
we call GENESIS simply *In the beginning*.

In the beginning God created the
heaven and the earth.

The earth had no form and was empty,
and darkness covered the face of the deep,
and the Spirit of God moved over the
waters and God said: "Let there be light."
And there was light.

And God separated the light from the
darkness and called the light Day and the
darkness Night, and there was evening
and morning, one day.

And God said: "Let there be a Firmament in the midst of the waters and let it
separate the waters from the waters." And
God called the firmament Heaven. And
there was evening and morning, a second
day.

And God said: "Let the waters under

the heavens be gathered together into
one place and let dry land appear." And He
called the dry land Earth and the waters
that were gathered together He called the
Seas. And God said: "Let the earth bring
forth vegetation, plants yielding seed and
fruit, trees bearing fruit. And there was
evening and morning, the third day.

And God said: "Let there be lights in
the firmament of the heavens to separate
the day from night, and let them be for
seasons and for days and years." And God
made two great lights, the greater light
to rule the day and the lesser the night.
And there was one evening and one
morning, a fourth day.

And God said: "Let the waters bring
forth swarms of living creatures and let

birds fly above the earth." And God blessed them saying: "Be fruitful and multiply." And there was one evening and morning, a fifth day.

And God said: "Let the earth bring forth living creatures and beasts of the earth."

And God said: "Let us make man in our image and let them have dominion over the fish and the birds and over the cattle and over all the earth."

So God created man in His own image. And it was evening and morning, the sixth day.

And on the seventh day God finished His work and rested. So God blessed the seventh day.

And in the day when He made the earth He took the Man and put him in the Garden of Eden and the Lord God said: "It is not good for Man to dwell alone. I will make a helper for him." And He made a woman and called her Eve.

## THINGS TO DO

Read the story of Creation in the first Chapter of Genesis. Write down some of the things God created.

# ROSES OF THE BIBLE

No 'real' roses, as Europeans know them, grew in Palestine except on the Lebanon, but the word occurs in various books of the Bible.

1.
The PHOENECIAN ROSE (Esdras* 2. Chapter 2; 19) is very like the English wild rose. It grows up to nine feet and its long branches have hooked thorns. The leaves are a yellowish-brown and the sweet-smelling flowers are white. There can be as many as forty flowers on one branch.

2.
ROSE OF SHARON (Song of Solomon 2; 1) is really a type of tulip. It grows wild on the plain of Sharon (between Mount Carmel and Joppa) and makes a wonderful sight after the spring rains, with its glowing red flowers.

3.
ROSE OF ISAIAH (35; 1–2). The Hebrew rose is a bulbous flower and not a tree. It is a NARCISSUS. The word NARKON (narcissus) was wrongly translated as ROSE.

4.
In Ecclesiasticus* we find the rose once more, (39; 13). Scholars say this rose of the brooks is the oleander, the rhododendron or 'rose bush' of the Greeks. It can grow to twenty feet and likes to be near wells or streams. The flowers are red, white or even purple. In Spain it is called the laurel. It is very poisonous.

5.
The ROSE OF JERICHO is a very strange 'rose'. It has a funny name, which suits it, for it is named 'the rolling thing'. It is a plant that looks like a dried withered ball when it is found on the plains by the Dead Sea. Sometimes it is called the 'Resurrection' flower. The 'ball' is blown about by the wind until it comes to rest somewhere and with a little moisture it takes root again. Its dried stems unroll, tiny flowers and fresh green leaves appear and the whole thing lies flat on the earth.

**Note**
*Esdras and Ecclesiasticus are not found in your usual Bible. They are in the Apochrapha.*

# BIRDS OF THE BIBLE

Can you fit the verses to the right picture?

1.  He's a very odd bird with a very big bill
    And a pouch underneath which he likes
      to fill
    With breakfast and dinner of carp and
      bream,
    Which he will then leisurely eat, it
      would seem.

2.  The . . . wears spectacles, so I have
      heard,
    He's certainly known as a very wise
      bird.
    He feeds upon young things like birds,
      mice and rabbit,
    And flies in the night which is not a nice
      habit.

3.  The . . . . . . . is a handsome male
    with gorgeous trailing tail,
    But how it glitters, how it glows
    When wooing. *How* his beauty shows!
    Yet Mother P. is very plain
    So Mr. P. has much to gain.

4a. He sails, just like a noble boat,
    Or pure white galleon.
    In England he's a royal bird,
    Which none may shoot upon.

4b. There is a childish story,
    A DUCK, the people said,
    But when he grew the watchers knew
    He was a . . . . instead.

5.  My love, my love, my little love
    The . . . . . . coos in rocks above,
    In Palestine so poor its price
    'Twas used by most in sacrifice.

6.  Great wings outstretched in majesty,
    The . . . . . . . . . . . . . . folk would see,
    And marvel at the awesome sight—
    Though sorry for its poor prey's plight.

*Answers on page 126*

10

# NOAH AND THE ARK

Noah stood considering the great ark he was building. It was strange to make a sort of *boat* in the middle of a grassy field. He shook his head, wondering about it all. But it was the Lord's command and Noah, in his simple way, could only obey.

But it wasn't pleasant when the villagers gathered round each day to jeer.

"Noah, when is the boat going to sail?"

"Tell us, old man, how will it sail on sand and grass?"

"He's mad!"

Noah didn't lose his temper very often. The villagers just didn't understand. How could they when they didn't know the Lord? If they believed in Him they'd lead better lives. Noah and his family were the only ones who listened to God's voice and tried to obey Him, and even his own family sometimes questioned Noah about the ark. *Why* was he building it? How could it *sail*—if it were *meant* to sail?

The old man couldn't explain; he simply said that he was obeying the Lord and they must leave it at that.

Sometimes he *did* try to get the villagers to be more respectful, for when they mocked him they were mocking the Lord's commands.

He looked now at the sky. It was cloudless—like a great blue sea, Noah would have said, if he had ever seen an ocean. It had been cloudless ever since he had started to build the ark.

But now it was finished down to the smallest detail.

Mark you, Noah hadn't *invented* it. He'd had *instructions*. The Lord had said: "Make yourself an ark of gopher wood; make rooms in it and cover it inside and out with pitch. This is how you are to make it; the length of the ark will be 300 cubits, its breadth 50 cubits and its height 30 cubits. Make a roof for the ark and finish it to a cubit above; set a door in its side; make it with lower, second and third decks."

The Lord was going to save Noah and his family, but the wicked and evil people must die, with most of the living creatures.

It was all very strange, *very* strange. If He meant to save some creatures—how would they know where to come?

"The Lord has said it. He'll find a way," Noah said aloud, angry with himself for even *wondering* how it was all to happen.

He looked again at the sky. Surely that was a cloud in the distance? Surely it was growing larger and larger and coming nearer and nearer?

Yes, decided the old man as the sky became overcast.

He called his wife, his three sons and their wives.

"Oh, father," flustered Mrs. Noah, "I don't like to leave so much behind—anyone might take my things."

"The Lord will take care of us," Noah said gently.

There was a hurry and scurry of wings. Birds came, singing their hearts out as the first drops of rain began to fall. In the distance, coming ever nearer, they heard familiar—and strange—animal sounds and saw hordes of creatures, large and small, male and female.

The family watched them all enter the ark; Mother filled with horror, perhaps, as two huge elephants clumped heavily in or a couple of leopards moved in more gracefully.

"Look at the *birds*," advised Noah kindly. "They know they are safe in God's good care."

"We haven't your faith," whispered his wife.

"You will know the Lord in His own time," said Noah, and he hurried his family into the ark.

Now the rain was falling heavily and the darkness hid what had been their little farm. Soon it seemed as if the heavens opened and a great storm waged. Only Noah stood on deck, watching the water. At first it drained away; puddles appeared, and presently there was a sheet of water which sent the villagers climbing frantically to the highest spot.

"He didn't want to do it," sighed Noah. "He told me He didn't want to—but what else *could* He do when His people grew so violent and evil?"

He looked up to the black sky. "You are the Captain, Lord," he said. "Guide us where You will."

The ark rose as the waters mounted.

Higher and higher . . . day after day, day after day, until it seemed it would go on for ever!

Sometimes the ark tossed about like a cockle shell on the flood of water; sometimes it seemed as if it must capsize and everyone on board would perish. Then there would be calm and fear would die away.

Often the little family wondered if life on earth would ever begin again. Often Noah had to remind them that the Lord was their guide. In His care all would be well.

Then came a day when the rain abated. The sun struggled through and a patch of blue appeared . . . then the rain really *did* cease. The decks steamed in the hot sun and Noah and his family rejoiced. They held their faces to the wind that had swept away the rain, to the sunshine. . . .

"We will send out a raven," Noah decided. "If it returns we shall know it didn't find a resting place."

The raven flew from the ark, its black wings shining blue in the bright light.

"We have only to wait and see," Noah told his family.

But the raven returned.

Noah waited seven more days and released a dove. How white it looked as, cooing, it flew away.

It was evening when the dove returned to the disappointed family.

Noah had to chide them. God was still their captain.

"Haven't we been guided all this time?" he asked sternly. "Do you forget that we had no rudder, no tiller, nothing to guide the ark with? In seven days we will send the dove out once more. Until then we must wait."

A second time the dove was sent out and a second time it returned. But this time it brought a tiny olive sprig in its beak. Somewhere, a tree was growing again!

Then came a day when the dove, sent out, did not return. A day came when the ark was grounded on Mount Ararat, but still there was water all round them.

At last came the wonderful, wonderful day when the Lord told Noah to open the door and bid all the creatures return to their native haunts.

Noah and his family stepped out into a new world.

How good it was to see fresh green grass. How marvellous looked the smallest, and largest, flower.

Noah's three sons, Shem, Ham and Japheth, watched the animals bound away and the birds, with a burst of song, fly to distant trees.

"It's as if they'd never known us," said the son who had had most care of the feeding of the creatures.

"It is their heritage," Noah reminded him. "Captivity is not for them . . . so let them go, son, let them go."

"What are we to do now?" asked Mother. "We shall need a new house—"

"Yes," agreed Noah," but first we must thank the Lord."

An altar was built and a sacrifice made.

The Lord was pleased that Noah hadn't forgotten Him as soon as danger was past.

"I will make a covenant with you," He said. "I will set my bow in the sky as a promise that never again will I drown the world with floods."

There was a great silence as, from end to end of the world, or so it seemed, a rainbow shone.

"Thank you, Lord," said Noah. The moment of reverent awe was over, and Noah and his family left the altar to build a new home.

## DO YOU KNOW?

Ham was the father of Canaan.

Noah became the first tiller of the ground.

Scientists who have studied the Bible made a model of the ark to scale, using the measurements given in Genesis 6; verses 13–16. It was like a large roof covering the 'decks and rooms' rather than like the toy Noah's Ark of which children used to be so fond.

## THINGS TO DO

Find a picture showing a rainbow over fields or sea.

Name the colours of the rainbow.

Make a picture with the rainbow.

Every time you see a real rainbow remember that God still takes care of us however badly we fail Him.

his wife Sarah, his servants and his nephew Lot, set out to become nomads.

The map shows you their route. You will notice that Abraham came from 'the other side of the river' so he and his descendants were called Hebrews, which means just that.

Later Lot left the company to settle in a fertile place, leaving Abraham to go on the harder way.

After many adventures over the years, and many promises from the Lord, Abraham and Sarah had a son, Isaac. Once Abraham thought God wished him to sacrifice his dearly-beloved son. But as he was about to slay the boy the Lord's voice bade him sacrifice a ram instead.

Many years later Abraham, who wished Isaac to marry a girl who believed in the One God, sent his servant Eliezer in search of such a maiden. Eliezer did not want to undertake either the search or the journey, but he obeyed. At last he

# ABRAHAM, ISAAC AND JACOB

Abraham lived by the River Euphrates, where his father Terah had come from Ur of the Chaldees.

It was a fertile valley with palms for fruit and shade, grass for their huge herds of cattle, sheep, goats and even camels; fields of wheat, golden at harvest, and above all there was water. So Abraham was a very wealthy man.

The neighbouring people worshipped many gods, but Abraham and his kinsfolk believed in the One True God. Then Abraham heard His voice telling him to leave this lovely land, his home and kindred, in search of a new country where he should become the 'father of a mighty nation'.

So great was Abraham's faith that he,

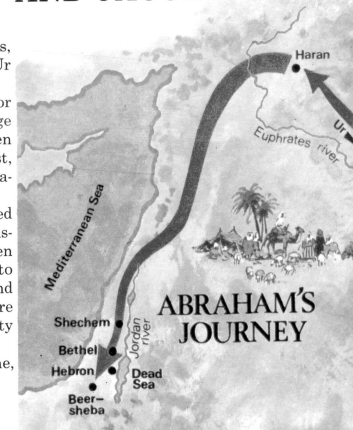

ABRAHAM'S JOURNEY

came within sight of 'Nahor's city' (Padan Haran) where he rested by a well.

Surely the Lord was with him, for out of all the people there, Rebekah, Bethuel's daughter and a kinswoman, came to water the flocks! Eliezer was taken to her home and welcomed joyfully.

Yes, agreed Rebekah, when they had heard Eliezer's story, it was the Lord's will, and she agreed to leave with Eliezer the next day. Her father blessed her as she left.

And Isaac went into the fields to meditate in the evening and he saw there were camels coming.

And Rebekah saw Isaac and alighted from the camel and said: "Who is the man walking in the fields to meet us?"

The servant said: "It is my master."

So she took her veil and covered herself.

And Isaac brought her into his tent and she became his wife and he loved her.

Rebekah had twin sons, Esau and Jacob. When they grew up Jacob tricked old Isaac into giving *him* the blessing which belonged to Esau, the first born of the twins, and he had to flee from his brother's anger.

Where did he flee? To his mother's brother Laban, whom he served for seven years in order to marry Rachel.

But now Jacob was to be tricked. Laban sent Leah, his older daughter, to Jacob's tent. She was heavily veiled and not until morning did he discover the trick. He served a further seven years for Rachel and eventually married her.

In those days a man might have many wives. Look at the Family Tree and see how many sons were born to Jacob, one of whom was Joseph.

## DO YOU KNOW?

Later the Lord told Jacob he was to be called ISRAEL, and in time Abraham's descendants were called 'The Children of Israel' or Israelites. Long years after, part of Palestine was called Judea, so for centuries now the Israelites have been called Jews.

# A FAMILY TREE

Have you ever made *your* Family Tree?

It is a list of your relations, and should go back as far as possible. Ask your grandparents who *their* parents were and if they remembered their own grandparents. Then make a list showing who married whom and how many children they had and so on.

There are people who make their living by turning up such information for people. They go to Parish Churches and study the registers and to graveyards to discover names.

Start with the names of Mum and Dad and *their* brothers and sisters. This will take up one line. On the line above put your grandparents' names and their brothers and sisters.

Then try to work back.

Here is Abraham's Family Tree.

Make the names of a few people in Abraham's family tree.

*Answers on page 126*

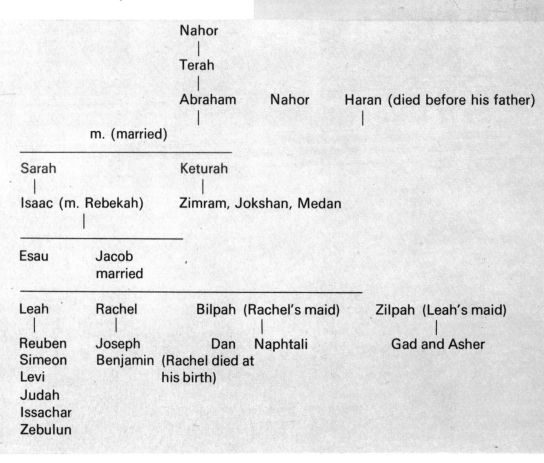

Nahor
|
Terah
|
Abraham     Nahor     Haran (died before his father)
|

m. (married)

Sarah           Keturah
|               |
Isaac (m. Rebekah)    Zimram, Jokshan, Medan
|

Esau      Jacob
         married

Leah     Rachel      Bilpah (Rachel's maid)     Zilpah (Leah's maid)
|         |             |                     |
Reuben    Joseph      Dan   Naphtali       Gad and Asher
Simeon    Benjamin (Rachel died at
Levi                his birth)
Judah
Issachar
Zebulun

# A DESERT SCENE

**Make this colourful Desert Scene. It isn't really difficult.**

Stand a shoe box on its long side. Paint the inside summer blue. When dry, paint low purple and brown hills along the bottom back, 1½–2 inches high.

**PALMS:** Take a strip of strong paper a little less than height of box by 3 inches wide. Colour ⅓ of the strip green on both sides; remainder brown, one side only. When dry, slit the green part into ¼-in. divisions, tapering the ends (Figure 1). Roll the strip into pencil thickness and glue trunk portion together. Pull down the green fronds. Slit the base for tabs. Make other trees of varying sizes.

**TENT:** Paint strong paper with stripes, 4–5″. Bend back ¼″ top and bottom and glue these to box side and floor. Fit a piece for tent opening or leave blank.

**FIGURES:** Draw your own or trace Figure 2, turning some left or right. Leave attachment tabs at base. Make recumbent sheep, all in proportion to size of box. Make a well, with tabs.

Lightly glue base and scatter sand, shaking off surplus.

Cover outside of box with neutral coloured paper.

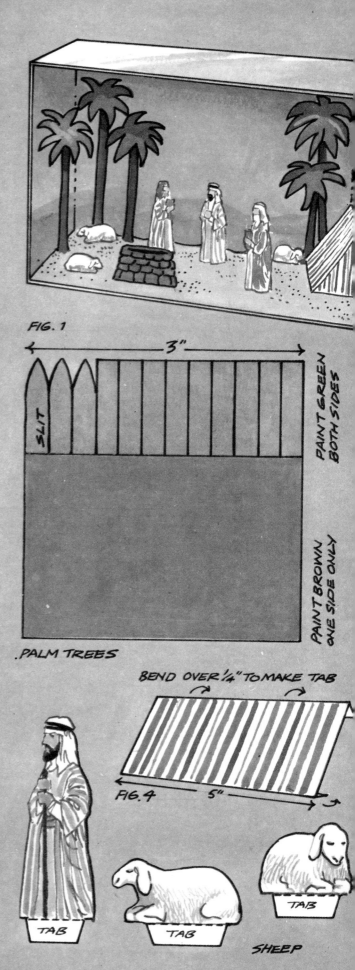

FIG. 1

PAINT GREEN BOTH SIDES

PAINT BROWN ONE SIDE ONLY

.PALM TREES

BEND OVER ¼″ TO MAKE TAB

FIG. 4    5″

FIG. 3. WELL

TAB

TAB

FIG. 2

TAB

TAB

SHEEP

# DO YOU KNOW?

Do you know that in the very early days of the Old Testament, long before Abraham and long after him, the people lived a pastoral life, tilling the soil. Noah is said to have been the first of the tillers. Esau, Isaac's son, and his brother Jacob represent the hunter and the farmer.

There were no settled religious Feasts such as the Passover, and no synagogues or Temples of the Lord. But the early beginnings of some of the agricultural feasts were there —the Ingathering, later known as the Feast of Booths and Tabernacles, started when people offered the first fruits of the harvests to their gods and later to the One True God. In many parts of the world to this day there are great celebrations and old customs connected with the gathering in of the grape harvest in particular. Many people in English-speaking lands have Harvest Festivals, which are similar in thought.

Do you know that Baal (Canaan-Phoenician meaning Master) was, they believed, the offspring of El, the father of gods, whose consort was Baalat (or Asherath, Astarte or Anath of the Old Testament). Baal was the god who looked after the crops and farm families. The worship existed when the Israelites began their journey into Canaan under Moses. Worship was conducted by priests in the field, and the people brought their offerings of wine, oil, first fruits and first born of the flocks. 'High Places' were sacred in Canaan, and by the time of Samuel we read of priest and prophet making use of such sites.

Do you know that by the time of Abraham —even before—the father of the family was both priest and parent. His words were never questioned. We hear of no struggle by Isaac when his father was about to slay him as a sacrifice to the Lord. The father of the family or tribe was also judge and was all-powerful. Long afterwards Hebrew prophets waged war against the worship.

*Barley. Hebrew: seorah*

The sketch shows you the method used in Egypt and almost certainly in Bible lands in early days.

Later rotary mills appeared.

When the Passover was instituted, leaven was left out of the bread. Today devout Jews eat MATZOS which look like dinner-plate sized water biscuits or very plain, round cream crackers.

OLIVES were greatly relished and when tribal life developed into individual homes almost every family had at least one olive tree.

EGGS poached in oil became a favourite item of food.

A traveller in the desert was always sure of a welcome; remember the story of Abraham and the strangers.

# FOODS OF THE BIBLE

People of Bible lands have always lived chiefly on vegetables and cereals (*not* in packets) with meat only on special occasions.

Do you remember how Abraham's servants were told to prepare *meat* for the strangers who visited him near the oaks of Mamre? You can read the story in Genesis, chapter 18.

On this occasion a calf was killed in honour of the visitors, but generally MEAT meant FOOD, not animal flesh.

BARLEY was the food of the poor people, but they were allowed into the fields to pick up any grain which fell during the harvesting.

Do you know there are at least eleven Hebrew words which mean *corn*, but wheat was the most prized crop. This was ground into flour, mixed with leaven (yeast) and made into flat cakes.

*Woman grinding corn. Egyptian statuette.*

## QUICK QUIZ

1. *What type of grain is most popular in Scotland?*
2. *What vegetable is popular in Ireland?*
3. *Chinese eat a great amount of ____.*

*Answers on page 126*

# INTERESTING ITEMS

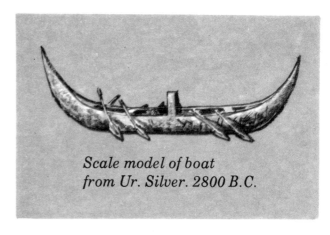

*Scale model of boat from Ur. Silver. 2800 B.C.*

**Evening.** The Israelites reckoned a day from one evening to the next. The evening was the important part of daily life and is often mentioned in the Bible. You will find this in the Creation story. The Jewish sabbath (Shabbat) of modern days is still reckoned in the same way, from sunset on Friday to sunset on Saturday.

**Blessings.** The Hebrews used many forms of blessings to fit various occasions. They were meant to bring good to those blessed. In very early Old Testament times the father, as head of the tribe and all-important, was able to bestow blessings; later, kings and still later, priests, became the bestowers of blessings. Here is a blessing which was given to the Hebrews so long ago and may still be heard in our Churches to this day:

*The Lord bless you and keep you;*
*The Lord make His face to shine upon you;*
*The Lord lift up His countenance upon*
*you and give you peace.*

Today, Jews wish each other 'Happy Shabbat'. See if you can collect some forms of blessing: Good bye = God be with you.

BOATS. In Abraham's city of Ur a silver model of a boat was excavated. It must have been the type which Abraham would have seen on the River Euphrates. Abraham, like most agricultural people, made the journey from Haran to Canaan overland. The Israelites in Egypt often saw different methods of sailing—plaited wicker boats daubed with bitumen—did these give the mother of Moses her idea for the little 'basket'?—royal barges as well as boats of papyrus.

*Papyrus boat still used on Lake Chad.*

# JOSEPH AND HIS BROTHERS

Joseph leaped and raced along the hilly path. His cloak swung and swirled, for it was rather too big for him. He stopped and wound it round himself and walked along more slowly.

He was proud and glad that his father Jacob had given him the cloak, for it meant that one day he would be master of the tribe.

It had been woven in days gone by, with many pieces. It was a little faded now, but the big wide sleeves gave it its real importance. Of course if his father had married Rachel, as his father-in-law had promised Joseph would have been the first-born so really he was entitled to become the heir.

Joseph sighed.

The gift of the cloak had caused a lot of trouble already, because his older brothers—ten of them—were angry and jealous that Joseph, next to the youngest son, should be picked out by their father.

Joseph had been rather stupid telling them about his dreams, even though he had known quite well that the telling would anger the brothers.

"I dreamed a dream. We were binding our sheaves in the field and my sheaf rose and stood upright and your sheaves rose and bowed down to mine."

How angry his brothers were. "Shall you reign over us?" they asked, "and shall you be master?"

There had been another dream which had made his parents angry, for in the dream he had seen the sun and moon and eleven stars bow down to him. His father

23

had rebuked him: "What is this dream you dreamed? Shall I and your mother bow down to you?"

Now he was on his way to see his brothers. His father had sent him to their encampment at Shechem to see how they were faring.

The brothers had seen him in the distance.

"Look," said one, "there is a cloud of dust yonder, and yet no wind to raise it. Someone must be coming this way."

The men gathered together. The advent of any stranger made a pleasant break in their enforced absence from home. But was it friend or foe?

"It's a man!" exclaimed Simeon as the dust settled and Joseph came into sight. "No it isn't—it's a youth—"

"It's JOSEPH!" said Dan. "Joseph in our father's cloak."

"*Joseph*! Skipping about like a goat let out to grass," said Issachar. "Our father shouldn't have given the cloak to him."

They watched their brother climb the rocky hillside. How they *hated* him! If only he would slip from the rocks and fall to his death.

At last one of them said what was in the minds of most.

"Let us kill him!"

Only Judah and Reuben refused to join in such a plot.

Reuben stepped forward.

"No," he said, "you must not kill him." He stared at the others and hurried on: "You could throw him in yonder pit instead."

And then, he thought, I can get him out and send him off home when the others are away or asleep. The pit is dry, the lad will come to no harm except a bump or two. Judah and he would be powerless against the others. Reuben left them to it; he would return.

Reuben was the eldest and in those days people were taught to respect their elders. So, for the time being, the others pretended to agree—Joseph could be disposed of when Reuben and Judah were not about.

Joseph drew near and called merrily. "I have come with news of our father and mother. They wish to know how you fare."

He got no further.

"We fare no better for your visit," said one, as the others seized the youth.

"Ho, dreamer," mocked another, "have you had any more dreams?"

"Have you dreamed what's going to happen to you now?" scoffed another as they dragged him towards the pit.

Joseph screamed and struggled like a mad thing, but in vain. He was flung into the pit and lay at the bottom, half stunned.

His brothers went back to their earlier pursuits, but they were quieter now, because, deep down, each was ashamed.

Joseph was also quiet.

Had the fall *killed* him?

The men sat uneasily on the bank, hardly daring to look at each other.

Judah broke the silence.

"Look," he said, pointing to the distance, "here comes a travelling company. If they are merchants we might sell Joseph to them. It will do no good to kill him. He is our brother."

"That's a fine idea," sneered one, "and as soon as the story gets about—what then?"

"Foreigners won't know what he says,

and if they do who would believe his
story?" answered Judah, obstinately.

"It would be wiser to kill him," said
another.

"He is our brother," insisted Judah.

The men looked at him. Reuben was
against them. Soon there might be more
than two against the rest. Yes, they
agreed, they would sell Joseph and that
would be the last of him.

So it was settled, and while one went
to hail the merchants others hurried to
the pit to get Joseph out.

He was half stunned, and hardly knew
what was happening as he was dragged
along towards the strangers.

The merchants looked at the youth.
He wasn't up to much but they would give
twenty pieces of silver for him, no more,
they said with signs and a few halting
words.

The brothers took the money, tore off
Joseph's cloak and shoved him towards
the merchants.

Now Joseph understood only too well.
He was to be sold as a slave!

He began to fight and struggle, scream-
ing for mercy, but his brothers struck him
and the strangers tore him away when he
would have clung to those who hated
him.

"See, Joseph," jeered one brother,
running along by Joseph's side as he was
hustled away, "see, we bow down before
you!" He waved the cloak. "What will
our father say when we tell him that a
wild beast has devoured you?"

But Joseph heard no more. He was on
his way to a strange land. His cuts and
bruises hurt him; he was lonely and
frightened, but of one thing he was sure—
the God of his father would be with him,
however bad things seemed to be.

He couldn't understand why he must
suffer so, but he would trust in God.

So Joseph came to Egypt.

Egypt, interpreted the dreams of two fellow prisoners. Then Pharaoh, who was also troubled by dreams, asked for Joseph's help. Joseph interpreted his dreams and so saved Egypt from a great famine which spread into the neighbouring countries.

Thus the youth, who had been sold as a slave, became a rich and powerful member of Pharaoh's court.

When Joseph's brothers came to Egypt to buy corn, they did not recognise him, though he knew them. Joseph was able to play a series of tricks on them, putting them through many trials before he revealed his identity.

Then Jacob and his family were sent for, and father and son were reunited with great rejoicing.

Meanwhile Reuben had returned to get Joseph out of the pit. He turned on his brothers when he found he had come in vain.

"What have you done with the boy?" he demanded. "If you have killed him our father shall know about it."

"Alas, alas," they said, "a wild beast got into the pit and we couldn't save him, however hard we tried . . . and here is his cloak—stained with his blood." And they showed Reuben the cloak stained with the blood of a kid they had killed.

When they returned home their father Jacob wept.

"I shall mourn for Joseph all my life," he said.

But Jacob did see Joseph again.

Joseph, when he was imprisoned in

# SPICES OF THE BIBLE

**"And the Lord said to Moses: 'Take sweet spices, stacte and onycha and galbanum, sweet spices with pure frankincense, of each there shall be equal part, and make an incense . . .'"**

Exodus 30.34–35. (R.S.T.)

*Stacte* means gum, which runs from certain trees. Here it refers to *Storax*, a beautiful shrub which can reach the growth of a fair-sized tree.

Its blossoms are rather like snowdrops, waxen-white with bright orange anthers (the part of the stamens which contains pollen). In full bloom, about March, it resembles a snow-covered bush.

To get the gum a cut is made in the branches, and the gum flows out to be gathered in reeds. After hardening the stacte is scraped off in compact masses in which 'drops' occur. These are called 'tears' and contain resin and benzoic acid. In early days in England, storax was used in perfume pomades.

*Onycha* is a rock rose and gives a gum called labdanum. The flowers can be as large as three inches across, white, with blotches of vivid scarlet-rose. The name is Greek, meaning 'finger nail'.

The bush grows 3 feet across, unlike English rock roses, seen in rockeries, which are quite small.

Late in the year soft, sticky resin appears on leaves and stems. The Greeks claim it has medicinal powers. It was highly regarded in Biblical days.

A story is told that this resin was first discovered when a herd of goats, grazing among the onycha, went home with their long beards sticky with the gum which hardened in the air.

28

# PLACES QUIZ

1. Where did the Ark rest after the Flood?
2. Abraham crossed from 'the other side' of the River ………
3. He travelled into C…..
4. The land of Goshen was in N.W. E….
5. The capital city of Pharaoh was at ..
6. The Greeks called it H………
7. The first 'water rights contract' was probably made at B……..

## FIND THE STRANGER

| | a | b | c |
|---|---|---|---|
| 1. | Leah | Rachel | Zion |
| 2. | Jordan | Israel | Euphrates |
| 3. | Pharaoh | Joseph | Reuben |
| 4. | Beersheba | Shem | Japheth |
| 5. | Timbrel | tabret | tares |
| 6. | Shophar | trumpet | scrip |

*Answers on page 126*

## DO YOU KNOW?

Jebus was one of the names for Jerusalem before it was captured by David.

The first day of the new moon, the beginning of the lunar month, was observed as a holy day, with sacrifices, blowing of trumpets and abstinance from work. (Numbers 10.10)

MERCY SEAT. This was the cover of the Ark of the Covenant. On it knelt two cherubim, their wings outstretched. It was completely covered with gold.

HEBRON was a very old city, for many years the capital of David before he captured Jerusalem.

# A PELICAN GREETINGS CARD

You can make this Pelican Greetings Card.

Move lever (Ba) right and left
and the beak will open and close.
Write your greetings at B.
**Materials:** Card 14″ x 5″
strip 2½″ x 6½″ (beak leaver, B.Ba)
brass paper fastener (eye and attachment)
black waterproof ink (optional, but
gives professional touch)
pencil and paper
ruler
brush
paints: orange, green, brown
scissors

**Method:** Square Sketch A. Fold card to
make 5″ x 7″ and lightly square the front and
copy the design square by square. Cut out.
B. Slit the beak x-x and the card d-d (careful
now). Slide B through beak slot and the d-d
slot. Fasten eye hole with paper fastener
through b and b and turn back the prongs on
the underside of the card. If this fits, remove
and paint the beak and greetings (or you may
pack the pouch with fish) replace and paint
the front of the card A. Close three open sides
of the card with glue.

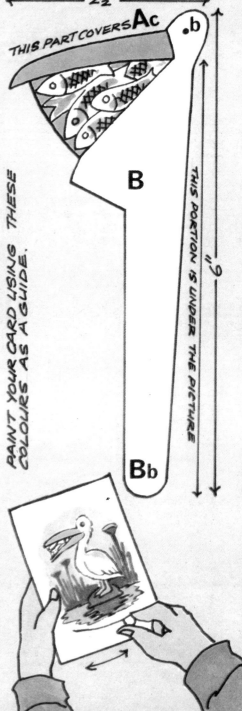

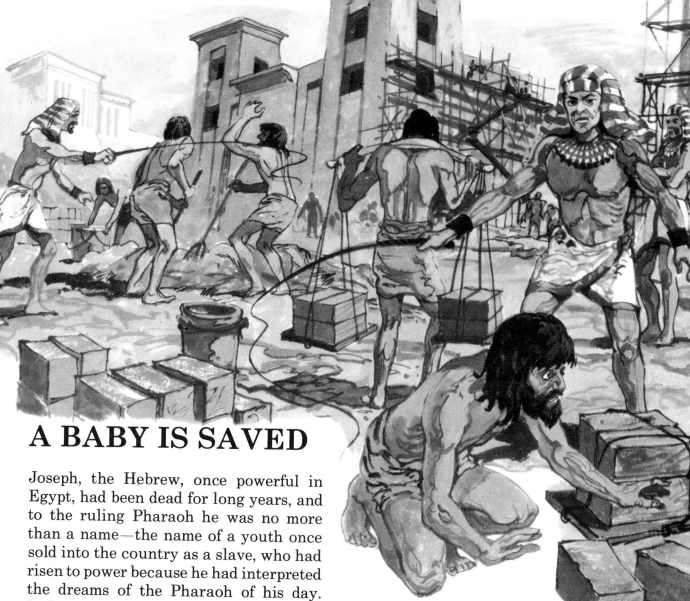

# A BABY IS SAVED

Joseph, the Hebrew, once powerful in Egypt, had been dead for long years, and to the ruling Pharaoh he was no more than a name—the name of a youth once sold into the country as a slave, who had risen to power because he had interpreted the dreams of the Pharaoh of his day. In fact it was because of that power that he had brought his large family into Egypt. They had multiplied and now the country was overrun with Hebrews; they held key positions and if the opportunity arose they were strong enough, no doubt, to overthrow Pharaoh, whose own people would become slaves.

Pharaoh frowned. Something must be done. Every Hebrew should be dismissed from office and sent to work in the vast brickfields. But even this, Pharaoh soon found, was of little good. Though unused to the back-breaking work of making bricks, trampling the wet clay, which had to be mixed with straw to bind it, in spite of having to spend hours in the blazing sun, the Hebrews continued to multiply

and the majority of babies born to them seemed to be males, and fine healthy boys at that!

Orders were issued to the effect that no straw was to be provided; the Hebrews must gather it for themselves and yet make as many bricks per man as before! Task masters were set over them, men with whips which they used without mercy on the bare backs of the miserable Hebrews. But still they multiplied.

Pharaoh consulted with his ministers. The male infants born to the Hebrews must be put to death in one way or another. Girls didn't matter. They could be married off to Egyptians or sold as slaves.

What desolation there was. The fathers in the brick-fields were dim-eyed with sorrow as one after another saw his infant son done to death by the sword or thrown into the river; their wives grew wan and silent, except for the few who dared to rail against Pharaoh or, sometimes, even the Lord God, who surely had deserted them!

Then a baby was born to Jochabed.

What a solemn-eyed infant he was, "as if he knew the fate that awaited him," wept his mother.

But certainly the Lord was guiding her, for after days and nights of torment, fearing the soldiers would discover his birth, she decided to drug the child with herbs and make an attempt to keep him hidden.

For three months the baby thrived in safety until his sleepy cries grew louder and his discomfort more obvious, and his mother knew she could not hope to hide him much longer.

Then inspiration came.

She recollected that every day the daughter of Pharaoh and her maidens would come to the river to wash. Suppose she made a little ark for the baby—hadn't Noah once saved *his* family in an ark, though this one wouldn't be made of gopher wood—and suppose the princess found the child and took compassion on him?

She bade her daughter Miriam collect reeds from the river bank. Then she wove a basket, just large enough for the child, with a cover to match. She daubed it inside and out with pitch and when it was ready she filled it with dried grass. Then she put the baby in it and closed the lid, and just before daybreak she and Miriam went to the river. It was secluded here, and near enough for the princess to reach. Great reeds and golden flag-iris made a good curtain to shield them from the public eye.

With a fervent prayer Jochabed placed the basket in the shallow water near the fringe of reeds. Then she went over the plan which she and Miriam had discussed so often. The girl was to hide in the reeds—she would be well concealed—but if the princess found the basket and looked inside it, Miriam must go forward and say her part.

With a hurried blessing the mother left. Miriam would be safe from any passer-by and yet could distract attention from the floating cradle. What was unusual in a peasant girl gathering reeds?

It was not a pleasant task for a young maiden. When a night owl hooted Miriam started in fear; when the frogs croaked she jumped, startled; but as day broke her fears diminished and she waited hopefully.

At last she heard the laughter and chatter of Pharoah's daughter and her maidens, and little squeals as they stepped into the water. For a few minutes they stayed near the edge, the hot sun blazing down until the shallows warmed and then they ventured into deeper water.

Presently the princess moved towards the golden iris; she would gather an armful even if they were to be tossed away later. But as she stretched out her hand she stopped as she saw the basket among the rushes.

She bade her maidens draw it out. Fearfully—for who knew what it might contain—they brought the basket free of the reeds, took it to the water's edge and timidly lifted the lid.

"It's ... a ... *baby*!" gasped the princess, "a little Hebrew baby!"

She poked a finger at it, gingerly. The fresh air had swept away the cobwebs of sleep and drug and the infant blinked, screwed up his face and cried loudly.

At the sight of his tears the princess was filled with compassion.

"Do you know your fate if I leave you here?" she asked, picking him up. His small fingers clutched at her necklet,

pulled at her hair, and she laughed delightedly at her new toy.

"You shall be mine," she decided, speaking aloud. "We must get a Hebrew nurse for you and when you are old enough I shall bring you up as an Egyptian."

It was the cue Miriam had been waiting for.

Bravely she stepped forward.

"Oh, my lady," she said, "shall I find a Hebrew woman to be his nurse?"

The princess looked from the baby to the girl and summed up the situation.

"Yes," she said gently, "bring me a Hebrew woman to nurse him."

Miriam raced away to return with her mother.

"You will take my child and nurse him for me," said the princess. "I will pay you wages. As to his name, you shall call him Moses because I drew him out of the water."

Truly the Lord was gracious, thought Jochabed, as she returned home holding her baby tightly, but even *she* little knew of the work to which the Lord would call Moses years later.

He was to lead the Hebrews from bondage in Egypt, and to give the Law to them in the Wilderness . . . a Law which the Jewish people reverence to this day and on which many of our own laws are based.

You will find the full story in Exodus and a very wonderful story it is.

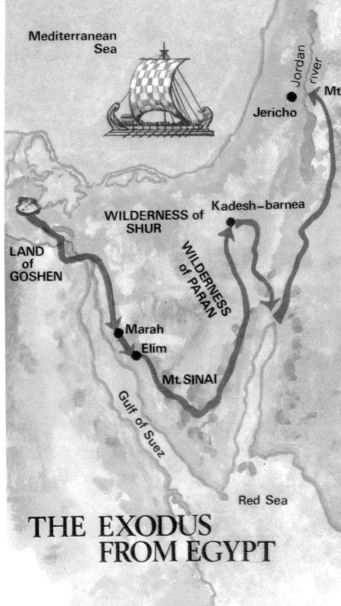

# THE EXODUS FROM EGYPT

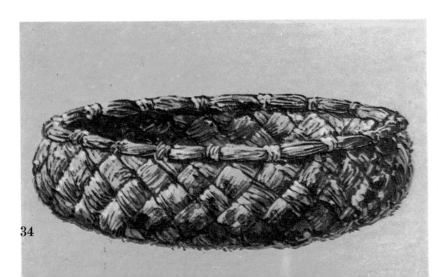

*Exodus seems to describe what is probably a wicker basket which people of the River Euphrates region make to this day. Crushed reed or papyrus stems are woven to make huge round or oval baskets. Gaps are plugged and the whole daubed with pitch.*

# ANIMALS OF THE BIBLE

**ASS.** In Bible lands a man's wealth was reckoned by the size of his herds. Abraham had 'sheep, oxen, he asses and she asses' in such herds that his men and those of his nephew Lot fell into bitter competition for wells and pasture.

The ass was far from stupid and could find a path which a man might think impossible. He was better than a horse for transport, because he needed less food and water and could carry a heavier load. The ass is believed by some to have originated in Abyssinia and was 'first cousin to the zebra'. He appears in Sumerian art as early as 3000 B.C. He was at work long before the camel. Even a poor man hoped to possess at least one ass. The white ones were considered fit for royalty.

The **CAMEL**. Scholars say that many of the Bible *camel* breeders were, in fact, breeders of *assess*, though we hear of camels later, after 1500 or 1000 B.C., although wild camels were known in ancient times in North Africa and Arabia. Once it was domesticated the camel was invaluable for transport in the fields, its milk (its flesh was forbidden as food: Leviticus 11.4) and its hair, clipped in summer, made fine cloth, its hide was used for shoes and its manure made into cakes for fuel.

**BEARS.** The Syrian bear is a light-coloured variety of the brown bear and was found in ravines of Galilee and Mounts Hermon and Hebron.

David told King Saul, in an attempt to prove he could kill Goliath, that he had killed a bear with his own hands when it had threatened his father's flocks.

**GOATS.** Every family owned a goat and could almost live from its produce. The goat belonged to the sheep family, to which it was closely related. The male was bearded and its horns were different from those of the female.

Goats' milk was much valued. Other products were: hair for tents and cloth, curtains and pillows (1 Samuel 19.13) meat and cheese; its skin was used for water bags.

**SHEEP.** In Bible days every family hoped to buy at least two lambs at Passover time. One was killed and eaten in the festival celebrating the safe exodus from Egypt, the other grew up as a playmate for the children, to become a source of clothing and wool for their looms. The pet lamb ate and slept with the children and even drank from their cups (see the story of Nathan, 2 Sam. 12.1–3). Sheep were intelligent and followed their master and answered his call.

**GAZELLES** and wild roe lived in the mountains and one psalm tells of the 'hart panting after the waterbrooks'. They were counted as 'clean' animals by the Law and fit for food. Egyptians living about 1375 B.C. made family pets of gazelles, and ivory statuettes of this animal have been found and may be seen in some museums.

# THE TABERNACLE

The Lord told Moses to set up a Tabernacle in the Wilderness and He gave him very particular instructions regarding it. It was to be portable because the Israelites were journeying to the Promised Land and when they moved it would be possible to transport this 'Tent of Meeting'.

There was a courtyard surrounded by curtains held up by posts (A). Near the entrance was an altar (B) and a *laver* for the priest's ablutions (C). At the far end was the tent divided into two parts, the Holy Place (D) and the Holy of Holies (E). In the Holy Place was a table of acacia wood completely covered with gold on which stood twelve loaves of bread representing the twelve tribes of Israel. These were renewed every sabbath, those of the previous week being solemnly eaten by Aaron and his sons—who were priests—standing as they ate them. There was a golden seven-branched candlestick, or lampstand (F), and the altar of Incense (G). In the Holy of Holies stood the Ark.

The ARK was a special chest covered with gold in which were placed the two Tablets of stone on which were written the Ten Commandments, a pot of manna and Aaron's rod, which budded. In later days the Ark was housed in the Temple. Later still it was lost and the Holy of Holies remained quite empty. The Ark was a reminder of God's presence.

# "WHITHER THOU GOEST ..."

It was high noon. Naomi sat weaving yet another basket in the hope of making a few pence with which to buy a little meal. Outside Ruth was humming – a rather sad little song – and Naomi wondered yet again if she should have insisted on the girl remaining in Moab.

She sighed, remembering how, long ago, she and her husband Elimelech had found it difficult to eke out a living in Bethlehem, where ravaging hordes of Midianites destroyed harvest after harvest, bringing famine to the land.

Looking towards the blue hills of Maob, they had decided to journey there with their two sons, Mahlon and Chillon, to make a new home. They had been happy enough, clinging to their faith in the One True God in a foreign land among strange gods.

Then Elimelech and her two sons had died, leaving their widows and Naomi alone. She decided to return to Bethlehem alone. Ruth and Orpah would surely find husbands among their own folk.

But it hadn't been as simple as that, for the young women had refused to allow Naomi to travel to Bethlehem; they would go with her and care for her.

She had tried to dissuade them and finally Orpah had agreed to remain, but Ruth was obdurate.

Holding Naomi closely she had said: "Where you go, I will go and where you lodge, I will lodge. Your people shall be my people and your God my God. The Lord do to me and more also if aught but death shall part us."

It was hard for the two women to make a living in Bethlehem, and as it was the time of barley harvest Ruth resolved to join the gleaners in the fields. They were allowed to gather any grain that fell from the bundles. Naomi warned her that as a foreigner she would not be popular; indeed there might be rough men who would even ill-treat her.

But Ruth was not daunted. Naomi's near kinsman had not offered his protection. It was the custom for a dead man's next of kin to offer marriage to the widow, for a male child born to such a marriage would be considered as the dead man's own son, thus carrying on the father's line. But Ruth had not been offered this protection so, somehow, they must get enough grain for a little bread.

It was hard work bending down in the hot sun to glean even a few ears of barley, but she persevered bravely.

The fields belonged to Boaz, a wealthy farmer who soon noticed the poorly-clad but beautiful young woman who worked ceaselessly.

He called a servant.

"Who is the stranger yonder?" he asked.

"She is Ruth, a Moabitess who came with Naomi when their husbands died. She refused to let Naomi come back alone, and is now working to get a little grain. They are in a sad plight."

Boaz nodded and walked to the field where Ruth laboured.

"Hear me, my daughter," he said. "Stay beside the women gleaners and go only into the fields where they work. I will see that none molests you."

Ruth bowed to the ground and whispered her thanks. She gazed up at her benefactor. "Why have I found favour with my lord?" she murmured.

"My daughter," said Boaz kindly, "I have heard how you left your own land to care for Naomi. You do not know our customs; our God is not your god, but the Lord will reward you for your goodness."

"I am comforted," said Ruth. "You have been kind to a stranger."

"The Lord bless you," replied Boaz, leaving her.

Ruth rose. She must not read more than was intended into the gracious words. He was just being kind to a stranger.

The hot afternoon wore on and when the other maidens went for their humble meal Ruth followed, keeping her distance carefully.

"Come here and take some bread." It was Boaz. Ruth, startled, looked up to see him standing there. "You must be hungry. Let this wine refresh you."

She obeyed, gratefully, too overcome for words, and when the gleaners moved she followed quietly.

Boaz rejoiced to see that she took no advantage of his kindness, and told the reapers to let fall a little extra grain for her.

At the end of the day when she went home her thick veil, looped to form a carrier, was filled with rich barley! They would have enough for some days!

Naomi listened to her story.

"Boaz is a kinsman, but there is one nearer . . ." she broke off. "I hope you behaved modestly," she added anxiously.

"I bowed myself to the ground," Ruth replied, simply, "and thanked him."

"The Lord will attend to us," her mother-in-law said.

So Ruth worked in the fields until the last day of harvest.

Naomi said: "Tonight there will be much feasting and merry-making. When Boaz goes to his tent you must follow quietly and lie at his feet. When he realises you wish to speak, you must tell him how we are placed and how our near kinsman has not offered his protection. Ask him what we must do, for we have no other to advise us."

It was very late when the noise and laughter died away and each man went to his tent.

Ruth waited in the silence; then, tremblingly, she crept into the tent and lay down at Boaz's feet.

Would he be angry? Would he say she presumed on his goodness?

The silence seemed too great to bear and a little sigh escaped her.

Then Boaz spoke.

"What is it, my daughter?" he asked.

The whole story burst from her. It seemed easy to talk in the warm darkness. The man did not interrupt her. Even when her words died away he did not break the stillness for a moment.

"I will see to it," he promised.

At home Ruth and Naomi could only wait.

Would he compel the kinsman to offer his protection?

That might not be a happy solution in the years ahead.

Then news buzzed round the city. Boaz had called the elders and people together. They were to meet at the Gate where public matters were always discussed!

What a commotion there was! Men jostling and muttering, women trying to hear what was going on; later, perhaps, to retell the story to Naomi....

Boaz stood before the gathering.

"I am here on behalf of my kinswoman Naomi," he said, keeping an eye on the near-kinsman, who looked rather worried. "She has a small plot of land which belonged to Elimelech and her two sons. She is now ready to sell it. Will you, her kinsman, offer?"

The man shifted his position. What price would the land bring? Were any strings attached?

At last he mumbled: "I will buy the plot."

"But," continued Boaz, as if he had not heard, "whoever buys the land must take Ruth with it."

The kinsman scowled. "Then I will not buy it," he said.

"Very well," nodded Boaz, "then _I_ will buy the plot and _I_ will marry Ruth. All of you here are my witnesses."

The kinsman took off his shoe and handed it to Boaz as a sign that he renounced his claim.

"We are your witnesses," shouted the crowd, as Boaz returned the shoe to its owner.

"The Lord make Ruth like Rachel and Leah who built the House of Israel," shouted one.

"Let your house be famous," cried another.

What a grand wedding there was for Boaz and Ruth and how joyful Naomi was when later a baby boy was born to them. They little knew that the child, Obed, was to be the grandfather of David, from whose line came Jesus Christ our King.

# FACTS FROM THE BIBLE

**BASKETS.** The Israelites used many different kinds of baskets, but it is not easy to decide their size or how much each held.

The most common basket in the Old Testament was the *sal*, which was carried on head or shoulder. In this, breads were presented in the Sanctuary; the *dûd* was used for carrying fruit and merchandise and the *tene* was a provision carrier, possibly quite large. The *kelub* was an enclosed type, – many think it was a cage.

The *tebah* was a basket used by river people of the lower Euphrates and almost certainly it was this which was used for hiding Moses.

**ASH PAN.** In Exodus various vessels are mentioned which were intended for taking the ashes from the altar – not the wood ashes, but pieces from the sacrificial offerings, and for taking away the charred wicks from the sanctuary lamps. The former were of bronze, the latter of gold. There are different names in Hebrew for these. See Exodus 27.3;38,3.

**BATHS.** It may surprise you to know that though baths were usually taken in a river or other suitable piece of water, some wealthy people had bathing installations built in their homes.

During excavations in Palestine a bathroom of about 2000 B.C. was brought to light. It was not, of course, like our modern bathrooms, though the Romans, at a later date, really did own very grand bathrooms.

The Tabernacle of Moses had a *laver* in which the priest had to bathe before he performed the service.

A man was supposed to wash his whole body before meeting a superior and the washing of one's feet was an everyday practice. The first duty of a host was to offer water and towels to a guest. Genesis 41.14 mentions that Joseph "shaved and changed his clothes" before his interview with Pharaoh.

42

**CHARCOAL.** You will have seen sticks of charcoal in the Art room at school or college, but – do you know – whenever *coal* is mentioned in the Bible it means *charcoal*.

Coal was unknown in Bible days.

There are three words in Hebrew to differentiate - (1) meaning black charcoal; (2) glowing charcoal; (3) half-burned embers.

The roots of broom give good charcoal. It is still sold by Arabs to this very day.

**CAMELS' HAIR** was used in very early days for the making of 'cloth'. The hair was clipped from the animal's neck, back and hump and woven on hand looms. The 'cloak' of Patriarch or wealthy shepherd, when made from camels' hair would last a lifetime. It was a protection against heat, cold or rain and sometimes served as a 'carpet' or even a tent!

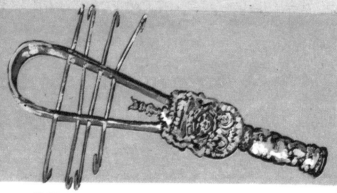

**THE SISTRUM** (plural sistra). When the Ark was first brought to Jerusalem, David and all the people 'danced before the Lord' and sang to the accompaniment of sistra and other instruments. This is the only mention in the Bible of sistra, which was a percussion instrument. The Egyptians, however, were very fond of it and it is often shown on monuments of the land.

**SPELT.** The Hebrew word is found three times in the Old Testament and in some versions is translated *rie*. Which word is used in *your* copy? (See Exodus 9.32).

It is a sort of poor quality wheat. Isaiah says that a wise farmer sows wheat and barley in his fields and spelt on the edges (Isaiah 28.25) but in some versions it says "cast in the principle wheat and the appointed barley and *rie* in their places." It is not *important*, merely of interest. Perhaps you will like to compare different versions of the Bible.

*Spelt* will grow on ground which is too poor even for grass! The Egyptians used it, and as this (and wheat) was a later crop it escaped the seventh plague. (See Exodus 9.32). Rie does not, generally, grow in Palestine. Perhaps early translators were puzzled as to what *spelt* actually was, and so used the word *rie*.

43

# RIGHT OR WRONG?

1. Genesis begins with the story of Moses.

2. Joseph had twelve brothers.

3. He had two dreams which angered his family.

4. All the brothers present wished to kill Joseph.

5. Reuben suggested putting him in a pit.

6. The brothers sold Joseph to merchants travelling to Arabia.

7. They were taking spices including balm and myrrh.

8. The merchants refused to buy Joseph.

9. Joseph rose to a high position in Egypt.

10. He never forgave his brothers.

11. He never saw his father again.

12. Joseph's 'coat of many colours' was important because it had long sleeves which denoted the position of master.

# JUMBLED FRUITS

## 1. PPLEA (TOCIRPA)

I am not the fruit most people know by this name, but a golden ball of soft delicious flesh, inside which is a hard nut. Prussic acid is produced from my kernel! When Solomon said "Comfort me with ppleas" (Song of Solomon) he was thinking of my revitalising perfume.

## 2. YARRBLCKEB

A prickly plant with clusters of small juicy purple fruits, I grow in Palestine and many European countries, where I may be gathered without payment. I am made into jam, jelly and used in pies. Arabs cut my branches with sickles to burn as fuel.

## 3. CCUUMRBE

I liked the thick moist mud of the Nile banks where I grew thick and plump, unlike my sausage shape of modern days. The Israelites enjoyed me in Egypt. Isaiah mentions a 'lodge of c............' which were cultivated in the Promised Land (Canaan). This was a rough shelter for the watchmen who, in the blazing sun, kept robbers away.

## 4. NOMLE

I am a cousin of No. 3. I am green with red flesh and black seeds. I have another cousin who is yellow and honey-sweet. Today hundreds of my family are sold by the Damascus Gate.

*Answers on page 126*

# A STORY OF SAMUEL

Samuel sat in a splash of sunshine which lay like a cloth of gold round the Ark, spilling over on the floor and making Samuel's white gown, or linen ephod, look quite rich. Soon the glow would die away and it would be night.

Samuel rubbed the brass lamp, although it couldn't have shone more brightly. He'd always cleaned it—ever since he had come to the Temple as a small child, and although he had other tasks this was his favourite.

The Ark was very holy. As long as the big, gold-covered chest stood there the people knew that God was with them, so it was right that the lamp should be well cared for.

He was so intent on his work that he did not hear Eli enter. The old priest's eyes were kind as he looked at the boy.

"Dreaming, lad?" he asked.

Samuel started and stood up. Then he sighed. Eli was old and liked a long night's sleep, but he, Samuel, was young and not ready for bed.

"You have taken a long time over your task," Eli continued.

"Yes," agreed Samuel.

He filled the lamp with pure vegetable oil, put in the trimmed wick and set it before the Ark.

"I was thinking how long it is since I came here," he said. "You asked me to polish the lamp that first time when you saw how near to tears I was."

"You were young to be taken from a mother's care, but I have tried to be father and mother to you," said the priest. He sighed, thinking perhaps of his own sons, Hophni and Phineas, who caused him so much pain.

Samuel pulled at the old man's gown.

"Sit down, my father," he begged, drawing up a bench and urging him to it. "Sit by me for a moment or two and tell me how you first met my mother."

Eli's eyes twinkled.

"You want to trick me into letting you stay up longer," he said, sitting. "But it is right that you should remember the story of how your mother gave you to the Lord."

He glanced around the humble Temple. Someday there would be a fine building to house the Ark, so big that all Israel would come to it with their offerings to the One True God.

But Eli did not know that.

"It's so long ago," he said slowly," and I have told you so often. I remember coming in one Feast Day and seeing your mother. Everyone outside was making merry, eating and drinking and shouting, for it was the Ingathering of the autumn fruits; but she was alone, her lips moving but saying no words."

"She was praying to the Lord," interrupted the boy.

"I thought she had taken too much wine and I was angry that she should come into the Lord's Temple like that," Eli said. "I went to her: 'Put away the wine from you,' I said. But she told me she was a sorrowful woman and had drunk neither wine nor strong drink, but had prayed with all her heart."

Eli paused, thinking back to that now distant day.

"Go on—go on—" urged Samuel, impatiently. "You always stop at the most exciting part."

"I was the answer to her prayer," said the boy to change the subject. "What else father Eli? You keep stopping."

"You know the story as well as I," grumbled the old man. He liked to take his time, and if he forgot small details what did it matter? The young had no patience.

"I will try not to interrupt again," promised Samuel.

"See that you do not." The priest frowned and then smiled at the boy's eager face. He continued the story.

"At first I did not recognise the happy smiling mother. She came to me and said: 'I am the woman who stood by you in the Temple, praying. I asked for a son and now I have brought him to the Lord. All his life he shall serve Him.' Oh, I remember her words."

"I saw then," continued Eli, "that she really had been praying very hard." He glanced round the Temple as though he saw her there now. "I did not ask her what she had prayed for. I simply said 'Go in peace and may the God of Israel grant your petition.' That was all I said to her."

Samuel sighed happily. He knew the end of the story quite well, but he never tired of hearing it.

"Time passed," went on the priest, "and I had forgotten all about her. Then one day I saw a man and a woman coming here, with a small boy skipping by their side. They were driving a bullock . . ."

"*Three* bullocks," corrected Samuel.

"Aye, three," agreed Eli. "And they had some measures of meal . . ."

"An ephah of meal," broke in Samuel.

"It does not matter whether she brought one or more measures," said Eli sharply. "The important thing is that she came back to thank the Lord. People are ever ready to *ask* but they are slow to give thanks."

The old man's head was nodding. Then with a start he glanced at the boy. "Your mother left you with me and though at first you were unhappy, we soon made friends . . . and I have loved you well."

"And I love you," nodded Samuel. "I like to work in this holy place."

"Someday, perhaps, the Lord will ask you to do greater tasks for Him. We shall see."

There was a moment's silence. Then Samuel said, half to himself, "I wonder if my mother thinks of me through the year until she comes to see me?"

"*Thinks* of you?" cried the priest. "How

could she weave an ephod for you every year if she did not?"

"Of course," agreed Samuel, laughing happily. "She could not do it without thinking of me often." He stroked the beautifully woven garment and added, "But I have other brothers and sisters now, and they must keep her busy."

"You are her first born and she has given you to the Lord," said Eli. "Would you wish her to regret her offering?"

"No, no," replied Samuel, quickly, "But it is good to know that I am not forgotten. How happy I am when she come to see me, when she and my father Elkanah make their yearly sacrifice. 'Why, Samuel,' she says, 'have you a new lamp here? It shines so brightly that it must be new!' Or else she looks about and says 'How clean you keep the Temple. Everything shines and sparkles'—"

"—or—" broke in the priest, "I think it is high time that Samuel went to his rest!"

He stood up, smiling, but Samuel knew he must obey.

"The Lord be with you, my father," he said, and Eli went out, leaving Samuel to get ready for the night.

"The young would never go to rest," muttered the old man, lying down on his couch.

Samuel smiled, pulled a blanket about himself and strutted to and fro.

"Shall I be bent and poor of sight when I am as old as father Eli?" he chuckled, bending his shoulders and pulling an imaginary beard, "and shall I have a great long beard?"

"When you are as old as I," called Eli, who, though deaf, heard surprisingly well on occasion, "I doubt if your beard will be one half so fine as mine. Go to sleep, lad, and stop chattering."

"Yes, yes," cried Samuel, hastily. "I will say my prayers at once."

He repeated words which he had learned from his mother and others which Eli had taught him, and then lay down, thinking of the next day when he was to play with a lad from the village. Would they go into the fields looking for wild honey or would they fish in the stream?

It didn't really matter—it would be fun whatever they did.

Then Samuel's thoughts turned to more serious matters as he remembered that his work was different from that of the village lads. He was set apart for the Lord's special work.

He repeated a prayer: "You shall walk in the ways that the Lord your God commanded you."

He grew sleepy.

Then, in the silence, he heard his name: "Samuel."

He jumped from his couch and ran to Eli calling:

"Here I am!"

The priest was asleep and Samuel looked at him, puzzled. Gently he shook Eli, who sat up, blinking.

49

"What is it, Samuel?" he asked.

"You called me."

"No, no, my son, I did not call," answered Eli. "Go back and lie down."

The boy turned and went to his couch. Perhaps he had dreamed it—or had Eli called in his sleep?

He said, softly: "There is none so holy as the Lord for there is none beside You, neither is there any rock like our God..." and he felt comforted.

As he lay down, conscious of the silence, he heard the voice again:

"Samuel!"

Once more he jumped up and ran to Eli calling: "Here I am."

Eli struggled up.

"Oh, Samuel, Samuel," he said. "When you were small and frightened of the night

"I did not call you," he said slowly. "Nay, my son, I did not call, but it seems to me that perhaps the Lord called you. You have not heard His voice, so how could you know it? Go back to bed, Samuel, and if you hear the voice again say: "Speak, Lord, for your servant hears."

He put his hand on the boy's head and blessed him and sent him back to his couch.

Samuel looked around.

The Ark was there, the lamp, not lit now, shone like gold. This was the House of God. Nothing could harm him.

He waited.

Then the Voice spoke as before.

"Samuel!"

This time Samuel was ready.

"Speak, Lord, for your servant hears."

What did the Lord say to Samuel?

It was a sad message, for He said that because of the wickedness of Eli's sons they were to be punished and because of this Eli, himself, would suffer.

Samuel was to become a great prophet and would anoint David, as a youth, and Saul, and so would begin the rule of kings.

owl's cry it was right for you to run to me, but you are growing older now and too big to disturb me so. Go back to bed, for I did not call you."

Samuel obeyed. He *had* heard the call, and clearly. He couldn't have dreamed the same dream twice in so short a time . . . He sat on the edge of his couch. Then he stood up and prayed:

*"The pillars of the earth are the Lord's
And He has set the world upon them.
He will keep the feet of His holy ones . . ."*

He lay down, repeating the words.

Again the call came: "Samuel!"

Really startled, the boy ran to the priest.

"Oh, my father," he gasped, half afraid to disturb Eli, "you did call. Three times I have heard you . . ."

Eli sat up.

## THINGS TO DO

Draw a scene from the story as you imagine it. Try to find a copy of the famous picture by Millais showing Samuel hearing the call.

Read the story in the Bible: 1 Samuel.

# RIGHT OR WRONG?

1. Samuel was the only child of his parents.

2. His mother's name was Hannah, his father's Elkanah.

3. The priest Eli found Hannah praying in the Temple at Jerusalem.

4. At first he thought she had drunk too much wine.

5. Eli scolded her.

6. He promised her she should have a son.

7. When Samuel was old enough his parents brought him to the Temple to 'give him to the Lord'.

8. Samuel never saw his mother again.

9. A linen ephod was thought to be an apron-like garment and part of the priestly dress.

10. Samuel heard the Lord twice.

11. He was brave and did not waken Eli.

12. Eli told him to answer: "Speak Lord, for thy servant listens."

## FIND THE STRANGER

| | a | b | c |
|---|---|---|---|
| 1. | Ephah | ephod | homer |
| 2. | Hannah | Elkanah | Phineas |
| 3. | Egypt | Shiloh | Bethel |
| 4. | Lily | lentil | lintel |

DO YOU KNOW there are no vowel points in early Hebrew writing. No wonder some words puzzled the translators of ancient writings.

Can you get these right?

1. Spk fr thy srvnt hrs.

2. Nd th chld Sml mnstrd nt th Lrd.

3. Nd l prcvd tht th Lrd hd clld th chld.

But there was a greater difficulty. No spaces were left between words! Try these.

4. MYHRTXLTSNTHLRDMYSTRNGTHS XLTDNTHLRD.

5. NDSMLGRWNDTHLRDWSWTHHMND LTNNFHSWRDSFLLTTHGRND.

*Answers on page 126*

# BRICKS

**". . . and Pharaoh commanded the task-master no longer to give the people straw to make bricks; let them gather straw for themselves."**

Exodus 5; 7.

There was plenty of stone in Palestine, but bricks were more generally used, perhaps because in very early times metal tools hadn't been invented and also because bricks were more easily and cheaply made.

In Babylon and Egypt the type of soils forced the inhabitants to use bricks for most of their buildings.

Look at the little copy of a tomb-painting showing the work. We have a great deal for which to thank those ancient tomb painters!

Bricks were made by trampling clay or clayey soil mixed with straw to bind it. In olden days in England—and elsewhere— plaster was mixed with horse hair for the same purpose; in art schools, students making plaster casts will put a piece of curtaining in the mould after part of the plaster has been poured in and before the final layer is added. This strengthens the work.

When the Pharaoh 'who knew not Joseph' set the Hebrews to brick making, he finally ordered that they must gather the straw for themselves and still make the same number of bricks. Corn was not cut at ground level, but near the ears. This was always burnt in the fields to give manure. The chopped straw was that which remained on the threshing floor after the trampling and winnowing of the corn sheeves. The Israelites had therefore to gather the stubble and make it fit for use in brickmaking, a great loss of time, making their work the harder.

# ACTIVITIES

1. Can you write a modern saying from the story of the Hebrews and their brick-making? It means we cannot make a good job without the right materials.

2. Another saying we have about bricks means we have said or done something embarrassing.

3. Do a project about bricks. This may be something quite different from anything you have attempted but it could prove very interesting. Begin with methods of brick-making in olden days and compare them with modern methods; compare the use of bricks with that of concrete. Why is the latter so much in evidence these days? Think of all the uses of bricks, from the garden patio to the very beautiful buildings which remain with us. Compare 'highline' blocks of flats made with precast concrete with the more gracious —but more expensive—a hint for you!— lower blocks of brick-built flats.

## NOTES TO HELP YOU

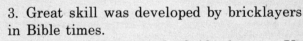

1. Mud or slime (probably bitumen in Mesopotamia) was used for mortar. Sometimes homes and shrines actually *dissolved* in prolonged rains.

2. Some sun-baked bricks have outlived 30 centuries, as at Ezion-geber (Tell el-Kheleifah). It was called the 'City of Bricks-with-straw'.

3. Great skill was developed by bricklayers in Bible times.

4. Houses of the period of Abraham at Ur have been discovered.

5. Rulers often had their bricks stamped with royal marks, some of which are still to be seen.

Now carry on. Bible Dictionaries are a great help. Have you any at school?

# PRAYERS FOR EVERY DAY

Teach me, good Lord, to serve Thee as
Thou deservest,
To give and not to count the cost;
to fight and not to heed the wounds;
To labour and not to look for any
reward save that of knowing that I do
Thy will. Amen.

The Lord give His Angels charge over
me to keep me in all His ways.
The Lord preserve my going out and my
coming in from this time forth and for
evermore.   Amen.

On getting up:
**Think of God and say:**

In the Name of the Father and of the Son
and of the Holy Spirit,
Amen.

**Thank Him**

Thank You, Heavenly Father, for taking
care of me during the night and for all
Your goodness to me. Bless us all.
Amen.

Don't forget the *Lord's Prayer* which you
say every day at home or at school.

Going to bed:

God be in my head, and in my understanding;
God be in my eyes and in my looking;
God be in my mouth and in my speaking;
God be in my heart and in my thinking;
God be at my end and at my departing.

# DAVID, SHEPHERD AND KING

"The Lord is my shepherd, I'll not want," sang David as he journeyed from his home in Bethlehem to the King's encampment on the hill which overlooked the valley of Terebinth. On the opposite hill the Philistines had taken up their position.

For some time, now, David had been King Saul's minstrel. His songs and poems and his magic way with his lyre were well known and when the king's dark depression – even frenzy – worsened, his advisers had suggested that the youth's skill might charm away the evil powers which seemed to beset Saul.

David did not stay all the time with the king. He was glad to be able to escape home to the sweet smell of the grassy places which were so refreshing after the close confinement of the tent, however royal that might be. Sometimes he even wondered if a *soldier's* life might be his in time to come... his song ceased as he remembered the day when old Samuel, the prophet and judge, had come to make a sacrifice with Jesse. He had asked Jesse to parade his sons before him. How puzzled his father had been, David reflected, as Samuel seemed to select – and then dismiss – one brother after another, finally asking if these seven were all the sons Jesse had.

"I have one son more," Jesse had replied, "but he is in the fields minding my flocks."

Samuel had asked for the boy to be brought and after the sacrifice had been offered, he had taken David aside – and that had appeared to be the real reason for the prophet's visit – for he had anointed the youth for future kingship, sternly bidding him to keep the knowledge to himself.

"It's strange," David said aloud. "Saul is king; I'm but a youth – how could I lead an army to battle, much less become a *King*?"

He shook his head. No use bothering about such mysteries – there were so many wonderful things in the world around him.

He sang again, the notes rising in the clear air as he went along.

"The heavens declare the glory of the Lord and the firmament shows his handiwork . . ."

Today David carried parched corn and bread for his three brothers, who were in the king's army and ten cheeses for the commander. There were those who considered that the youth wandered too freely among the soldiers – and asked more questions than any minstrel should. Even his brothers resented his presence.

"What is astir in the camp?" David asked as soon as he arrived.

"You were sent to sing to the king, not to ask questions which don't concern you," snapped Eliab, his oldest brother.

"I can't see why you're here at all," put in Abinadab, crossly. "You would be better employed minding our father's flocks."

As David moved away there was a stir on the opposite hillside. He stopped and turned.

There stood a man of such stature that David stared; a man clad in a coat of bronze mail with a bronze helmet on his head. As he moved, the sunlight glinted on the metal

57

so that it shone and gleamed until no man could fail to see him. Saul was a fine, broad-shouldered man who towered above most of his companions, but this enemy on the other side was a giant by comparison.

He swaggered from his ranks and shouted across the valley to the gaping Israelites, now gathered to face him:

"I defy the ranks of Israel this day. Give me one of your men to fight me single-handed. If he kills me, then my people shall be your servants and serve you, but if I prevail against him and kill him, then you shall be our servants."

There was a great silence. It seemed as if no man, on one side or the other, moved. Firmly the giant stood, as if alone, shining in great glory.

"Send me a man," he roared again, "that we may fight together."

He laughed mockingly; the echo was thrown back.

"Who is he?" asked David. "Why doesn't someone fight him?"

No one answered until a soldier said: "It is Goliath of Gath. Every morning and every evening he comes out to challenge us. Who is great enough to answer that challenge? Is one man to step out there for single combat – and deliver Israel into the hands of the Philistines?"

"Who is he who dares to defy the armies of the living God?" David persisted. "What shall be done to the man who kills this Philistine?".

"The king will give him great riches and the hand of his daughter in marriage," answered the soldier, "and will make his father's house free in the land . . . but what are great riches in the face of such danger?"

"Go back to our father's flocks," said Eliab, overhearing. "You just come to watch the battle. But there won't be a battle until Goliath tires of playing with us. He knows we have none to set against him. Go home, boy, and leave war to those who understand it."

"What have I done?" David asked. "May I not speak?"

He moved away.

A soldier, amused by the boy's questions, reported them to Saul. It was a comical story which might arouse the king from his dark mood.

"The Lord is my rock and my fortress and my deliverer; my God, my strength, in whom I will trust . . . " sang David. He broke off and spoke to Saul. "No one else will go against the enemy," he said. "Let your servant fight the Philistine."

The king looked at the slim young man and laughed loudly.

"Fight Goliath?" he roared. "*You?* You are but a youth and know nothing of fighting however sweet your music."

"When I kept my father's flocks," said David, "a lion came to devour the sheep, but I went after him and took the lamb from his mouth and killed him. Your servant has killed lions and bears, and this heathen Philistine shall be as one of them, for he has defied the armies of the living God."

Not all at once was Saul persuaded, but at last he told David: "Go, and the Lord be with you."

He bade his men put the youth into the king's own armour, but Saul was a huge man and David of smaller build, and he drooped under the weight of the heavy mail. What a spectacle he made as he staggered about, unable to walk because of the heaviness of the trappings.

Defiantly he faced the jeering men and took off the armour.

"I will go as I am, the Lord being my helper," he stated.

There were gasps as he walked from them, his staff in his hand, a shepherd's sling in readiness.

"He is mad . . . mad . . . " cried first one and then another as they watched him go.

"We shall all be butchered or thrown into slavery by the enemy," groaned others.

And yet they could not keep themselves from watching that fair youth going resolutely to meet a giant.

They saw him stop at the brook in the valley; watched him bend to pick something from the shining water, and stand, slim and erect, to face the raving giant who lumbered to meet him, shouting invectives at the insult shown.

"Am I a dog?" he bellowed across the valley. "Am I a dog that you challenge me with *sticks?* Come to me, boy, and I will give your flesh to the birds of the air and the beasts of the field!"

"You come to me with a spear and a javelin," shouted David, "but I come to you in the name of the Lord of Hosts, the God of the armies of Israel whom you defied.

This day the Lord will deliver you into my hand that all the earth may know that the Lord saves not with the sword and spear, for the battle is the Lord's and He will give you into our hands."

There was a silence. Then Goliath strode forward furiously, brandishing his huge, shining sword so that it struck fear into the watching armies on both sides.

And David put a stone of the brook into his sling and slung it.

The small stone hurtled through the air, swift and sure. It pierced Goliath through the forehead and he fell with a mighty groan.

Goliath was dead. The Philistines fled, pursued by the armies of Israel.

David became a great hero, but as his popularity grew, so also did Saul's hatred of the young victor.

David had to flee, to become an outlaw for many years, but at last, Saul dead, he was made King of Israel.

He was to conquer Jebus, the old city of *Urusalem,* and to make it – as Jerusalem – the capital of Israel; he was to set up a Tabernacle there for the Ark of God, but though he longed to build a Temple for the Lord, this joy was denied him.

He was a great and mighty king, a leader, a poet, but he had done so many evil things that Nathan, the prophet told him that the building of the Temple must be left to Solomon, his son.

# ODDS AND ENDS

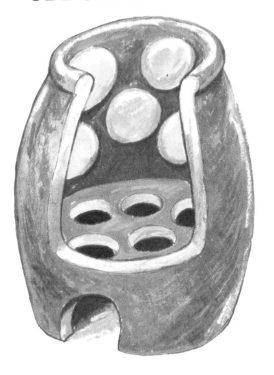

## BAKING

This is an oven. It was called a *tannur*, and was made of clay. It stood 2½ – 3ft high and measured about 15″ in diameter at the top to 24″ at the widest part. It had, usually, two compartments, the horizontal separator containing holes. The fire was made in the lower part and when the oven was hot enough, rounds of dough were skilfully stuck on the inner wall of the upper chamber. Part of the front has been cut away so that you can see inside. Sometimes the oven was buried in the ground or in a wall to retain its heat. A tannur like our sketch was found at Megiddo (or Megiddon) once an important city in north-central Palestine.

It is fortunate for us that the Egyptians carved or painted so many items showing occupations and that we have these in our museums.

Here we see two bakers kneading the dough in a huge container.

Here is a baker
rolling out the pastry.
He has a treadle to help
him in his task.

## HIGH PLACES

In Canaan ridges and elevated positions were chosen for temples and altars.

Long before the Jerusalem Temples were built, primitive people set up their shrines in such 'high places'.

In 1. Samuel chapter 10, verse 5, we read that a company of prophets were to be met 'coming down from the high place'.

In some of the high places where Jehovah (Yahweh) was worshipped, the feasts would occur nearby. After the fall of Judah we hear less of these 'high places'.

## HARP

1) **Kinnor.** The most ancient kind, of Syrian origin. It is a type of lyre of uncertain shape, but probably square or oval. It was made with pieces of wood united by 'animal' strings, of which there were probably six or nine.

2) **Nebbel.** This is a later improvement perhaps from Phonecea. It had three wooden sides, one carved. There were ten strings. If you come across the words **psaltery** or **lute** in the Bible, they will generally mean the **nebbel**. Students do not always agree and some claim it was a sort of dulcimer. It was used with other instruments and had either a base or shrill sound.

The **Israelitish nebbel** (sometimes spelt **nebel**) was played while walking. It is not often mentioned in the Old Testament, but in 1. Kings 10. 12 you will see that for the House of the Lord and the King's house harps and psalteries were to be made from the **Almug** tree, in 1. Samuel, 10. 5. "You shall see a company of prophets coming down from the high place with a psaltery, and a tabret and a pipe and a harp (nebel)." A **Tabret** was a kind of tambourine. (See also Gen, 31. 27. Isaiah 52. 12 for this last word). **Sackbut** was another kind of harp.

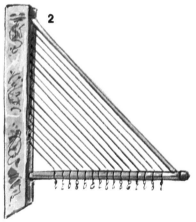

# ABIGAIL

Abigail stood in the doorway looking out at the fields, bright in the sunshine. There was the endless baa-baaing of Nabal's three thousand sheep as flock after flock followed their shepherds from Carmel to the shearing grounds.

Shearing time meant hard work in the house. The shearers and shepherds must be fed and there would be feasting for all. Abigail and her servants were busy baking hundreds of flat bread loaves; sheep had been killed and made ready; there were cartloads of dried raisin clusters, figs packed into 'cakes', skins of wine, and dozens of other delicacies for the hungry workers.

Abigail sighed. Were great riches and huge possessions compensation for life with Nabal, her drunken, brutish husband?

'Nabal' – the very name meant 'folly', but he was worse than a fool.

Suddenly she heard the sound of running footsteps and the breathless voice of Abda, one of the trusted servants.

"Oh, Mistress," he gasped, "oh mistress, we shall all be slain."

"Slain?" echoed Abigail. "*Slain?*" Have bandits come upon us?"

"Worse, mistress – David's men have been –"

"But David and his men *protect* farmers' flocks," protested Abigail. "Our shepherds have often said so."

She looked at Abda, puzzled. Everyone knew how David, now a fugitive from King Saul, lived as an outlaw. It was true that he often descended on a farm and asked for food and goods but what farmer begrudged him that when their animals were protected from robbers and marauders?

Abda was calmer now.

"Ten young men rode up as my Master Nabal was in the fields," he explained. "They greeted us in David's name: 'Peace be to you and to all your house,' they said. 'We hear that your shearers are at work. Your shepherds have been with us in Carmel, we gave them our protection."

"But why do you say we are in terrible danger?" interrupted Abigail.

"It was my master Nabal," began Abda. "He abused the men. 'Who is David, the son of Jesse?' he asked."

"Oh, *no!*" gasped Abigail. She understood, now. Such an insult must be avenged.

"He told them that servants were always

quarrelling and leaving their masters, and how was he to know that *these* men hadn't done so, and were trying to get food and goods intended for *our* servants? 'I'm not going to hand my provisions to you, just for the asking,' he said."

"They came in peace," said Abda, "and rode away in anger. David will surely bring an army and his vengeance will be terrible . . . ."

She looked past the servant to where others were busy in field and yard. David would not leave one living thing . . . "Saul has slain his thousands, but David has slain his tens of thousands," she quoted softly.

Yes, Nabal had gone too far this time. It would be the end of everything . . . everything . . . unless . . . *unless* . . . .

"The Lord will be with me," she said. "There is one way to save us . . . if the Lord is my guide . . . ."

Abda brightened. His mistress was wise.

"Call the servants," she said. "Say nothing to your master, but hasten. Then bring asses here, laden with baskets."

In a moment all was hustle and bustle.

"Fill the baskets with bread – at least two hundred loaves," she told one, and to another: "Bring a hundred clusters of dried raisins . . .

fill that basket with cakes of figs . . . bring wineskins, well filled . . . now parched corn . . . ."

The servants hurried to and fro until the asses were well laden with the best of the provisions.

"Now," she said, to her young man, "Go on before me on your asses and I will ride behind you. We will meet David and his army before they can reach us."

It was some time before they saw the glint of armour and heard the sound of galloping hooves, as David led his army along the mountain road.

Abigail ordered her men to stop.

Then she alighted from her ass as the army before her came to a standstill. David was amazed by the sight of this brave and beautiful woman coming towards him.

"My lord," she said gently, "let me bear the guilt of my husband Nabal's folly. I am your servant and did not see the young men you sent. As the Lord lives, as He has kept you from taking vengeance, do not seek revenge on us . . . my men have brought you gifts. Forgive the trespass of your servant, for the Lord will take his own vengeance, and you, my lord, will not be troubled by grief, conscience or the taking of blood . . . ."

David looked at her and was touched.

He smiled as he spoke softly to the woman: "Blessed be God who has saved me from doing terrible deeds today. Go in peace to your house. See, I have listened and heard your petition."

He gave the word of command to his men.

Slowly they turned and rode away.

I'm sure you would like to know the happy ending. David must often have thought of that beautiful, brave woman. In fact we know he did, for later he heard that Nabal had died and he sent for Abigail to make her his wife. Read the full story in 1. Samuel, chapter 25. to verse 42. Verse 43 may puzzle you, but remember, in those days a man might have more than one wife.

# THE NEW TESTAMENT

At the end of his Gospel, John said that Jesus had done
so many things which, if they were written down, even the
world itself could not contain the books that should be
written.
Like John, I also have only been able to include a few of
the wonderful happenings from the life of Jesus.

# The Annunciation

It was very beautiful in Nazareth at this time of the evening.

The work of the day was over, soon it would be night, thought Mary, as she walked in the shade of the olive trees.

She stood still, thinking of the Prophet Isaiah's words: "For every battle of the warrior there is confused noise and garments rolled in blood . . ." Would He be born in a palace to a great and noble princess and grow up to lead an army against the Roman Empire? And yet didn't the prophet say: "He shall be called the Prince of Peace"? That did not sound like one who would storm through the land, His path drenched with the blood of the conquered.

Mary sighed softly. Isaiah also promised: "The wolf shall dwell with the lamb, and the leopard lie down with the kid, and the calf and the lion and the fatling together . . . and a little Child shall lead them."

She smiled and looked into the distance. Soon the moonlight would turn the olive leaves to silver; but not yet. She would be home by that time; *now* it was still bright and sunny; the fields were a riot of purple, scarlet and cream with anemones − like the carpets from Persia which she had seen when merchantmen travelled that way, for though many didn't think much of little Nazareth, it stood near cross-roads, one of which led to Jerusalem.

Mary laughed merrily. The fields were more beautiful than any carpet woven by human hands; the Lord God had made those lilies of the field " . . . and a little Child shall lead them." He would be wonderful, the Counsellor . . . but first – a little Child. He would like small lambs and kids, yes, and flowers.

"They shall not hurt or destroy in all My holy mountain and the world shall be full of the glory of the Lord . . ."

A small breeze fluttered her veil; a tendril of dark hair escaped and she pushed it back.

The breeze whispered around . . . there seemed a radiance near the olive trees and Mary looked about her . . . and started back in fear, for someone stood there, someone serene, calm, beautiful . . . and Mary knelt and bowed her head to the Angel of the Lord.

"Hail, O favoured one, the Lord is with you."

She heard the words quite clearly. Favoured one? She, Mary, a humble village maiden?

She dared to look up, her eyes filled with wonder and puzzlement, as the Angel continued: "You have found favour with God, and behold, you will conceive and bear a Son and you shall call His name Jesus. He will be great and will be called the Son of the Most High and the Lord God will give to Him the throne of His father David and He will reign over the house of Jacob forever, and of His Kingdom there will be no end."

Mary gazed at the Angel and whispered: "How can this be, since I have no husband?"

"The Holy Spirit will come upon you, and the Power of the Most High will overshadow you, therefore the Child will be called Holy, the Son of God."

There was a silence, as if the whole world stood still, as if the Heaven of Heavens waited for her reply, for the choice was hers.

"A little Child shall lead them . . ."

Mary gave a small sigh. She was in God's hands. There was only one reply.

"Behold the handmaid of the Lord, be it unto me according to your word."

# SHRUBS OF THE BIBLE

**ALMOND.** This tree blossoms in the Holy Land as early as January. The fruit is wrapped in a heavy covering, wrinkled and leathery, which encases the shell of the nut. These nuts are used to produce oil. One hundred and fourteen pounds of fruit will give fifty pounds of oil. At one time the fruit was featured as the design on the shekel.

ALMOND   Hebrew: shaked

Hebrew: teasshur

**BOX** trees grow in the Lebanon. The leaves are much longer than the English variety. For centuries the wood has been used for making musical instruments, spoons and combs. It was a favourite with the Romans, who clipped it into shapes for their ornamental gardens (topiary work). In England, tombs going back to Roman times were found to contain sprigs of this tree, perhaps in place of myrtle, which was used in Italy for this purpose.

**SCARLET.** Its leaves are small and spiny and the bush is rather like a holly with acorns! Its young shoots are covered with soft down on which the kermes insect, *Chermes llicis* breeds. These insects give a beautiful scarlet dye. Sprigs were used in purification rites after a plague. When the bark of this oak is steeped in boiling water it gives a black dye which was used for dyeing hair. The Dyers' Company of England chose sprigs of this dye plant for their heraldic crest. It is still in use.

SCARLET
Quercus
coccifera
Hebrew: shani

CROWN OF THORNS
Greek: akontha

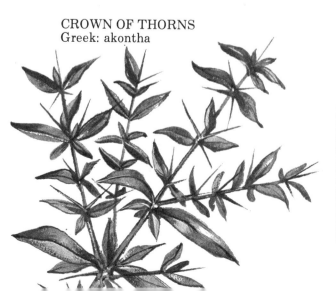

**CROWN OF THORNS.** Common throughout the Holy Land, this shrub was often dried for kindling. It is accepted by scholars as the shrub used by the soldiers to fashion the cruel Crown of Thorns which they placed on the head of Jesus. Tiny white flowers appear in spring.

# FLOWERS OF THE BIBLE

The Arabs speak of *sushan* and *hannum* to mean a pretty wild flower.

The term includes daisies, anemones and cyclamen, which for a brief season cover the hillsides where Our Lord often wandered. He might have meant any of these flowers when He spoke of the 'lilies of the field', but many scholars think it was the anemone, which grew in profusion, making a carpet of purple, scarlet, blue and cream. Even Solomon in all his glory wore garments no more beautifully coloured than these flowers.

The SAFFRON CROCUS grows wild in all the countries of the Levant. From its stigmas a powerful dyestuff is extracted. It is used in perfume and for flavouring.

It is mentioned in the Bible only once in the Song of Solomon.

**Can you fill in the missing words in these questions from the Bible?**

1. Behold the ..... of the heaven. (Matthew 6.26)

2. Consider the ...... of the field.

3. As a ... gathereth her ........ under her wing.

4. The symbol of God's Holy Spirit often appears as a ....*

5. What bird did Our Lord say could not fall to the ground without being noticed by God?

*'Tongues of fire' is also used as a well known symbol for the Holy Spirit, red being the colour for Whitsuntide, when the Holy Spirit descended upon all those gathered in the Upper Room, fifty days after the first Easter Day. A Bishop's mitre is shaped to remind us of the tongues of fire.

*Answers on page 126*

# CHRISTMAS NIGHT

It's quiet on the hillsides
For people are in bed,
Except such folk as shepherds
Who nod a sleepy head,
Or while away the hours
With stories or with song,
The fire will keep wild beasts away —
But oh! the night is long.

"How crowded were the alleys
And roads to Bethlehem.
Say, did you see that couple —
Did you pay heed to them?
A woman on a donkey —
A donkey small and brown;
The man — he walked beside her
But slowly — into town."

The others laughed, though kindly,
"The streets were crowded, man,
And many folk on donkeys
Were thronging every khan.*
How should we heed a Maiden,
Or man, or donkey brown,
When people in their hundreds
Were crowding into town?"

Then, as they chatted idly,
There shone a glorious light,
Which seemed to grow in brilliance
Till all the sky was bright;
And, standing in the Heavens,
An Angel hailed the men:
"All glory be to God on high.
Go you to Bethlehem."

The shepherds did not doubt him.
They ran to Bethlehem.
It seemed that the Messiah
At last had come to them.
And in a lowly stable
They found the Blessed Maid,
With Joseph standing silently
Where Jesus Christ was laid.

Right joyful were the shepherds
As each bent low his head
To worship Christ the Saviour
In humble manger bed.
"Oh, little Child so lowly,
Who came to earth for men,
Dwell in our hearts for ever,"
Whispered the shepherd men.

*Khan is the name for an eastern Inn.

71

# SOME JEWISH FESTIVALS

SABBATH

The **Sabbath** (Shabbat) was observed in Temple, synagogue and the home. Very special ceremonies are attached to this day, which begins on Friday at sunset and ends on Saturday at sunset. At first, for Christian Jews the sabbath continued to be observed as a day of rest, with Sunday, commemorating the Resurrection of Our Lord, a Feast Day. It is quite incorrect to call Sunday (the first day of the week) the Sabbath.

**The Passover:** A movable feast, falls on the 14th day of Nisan (March/April, the first month of the Jewish ecclesiastical year). It commemorates the flight from Egypt after the ten plagues. A lamb for each family was slain by the Temple priests, and was eaten with bitter herbs and unleavened bread. Jewish people of today do not kill a lamb, for there is no Temple. The Feast lasts eight days (seven in Israel) during which unleavened bread is eaten; on the second night a sheaf of corn was presented in the Temple at the beginning of the harvest before anyone ate of the new grain crop.

PASSOVER

PENTECOST – SHAVUOT

**Pentecost** (The Feast of Weeks; Day of the First Fruits falls on Sivan 6th, May/June). Fifty days after the sheaf offering, Pentecost is a harvest festival. People used to take gifts of fruit and corn to the Temple. Leaven may be used in the bread, for there was no haste connected with this Feast as there was with the Passover when, at its institution, the Children of Israel were prepared for hasty departure.

The Feast of Trumpets is held with simple ceremonies and synagogue attendance at the autumnal beginning of the Jewish civil year.

## FEAST OF TRUMPETS – NOWADAYS CALLED NEW YEAR

ANCIENT BOOTH

Feast of Tabernacles (or Booths) is observed at full moon in Tishri. It is a very joyful celebration nowadays. Jewish people dwell, for the period of the feast, in some type of erection through which the sky may be glimpsed. These huts or booths are decorated with paintings and pictures of Jewish scenes, paper chains in the shape of a *Magen David* (Star of David), lanterns and little coloured bottles of red, blue or green. Special ceremonies include the use of a palm branch, three twigs of myrtle, two twigs of willow and a fresh citron. The Festival starts on the 15th day of the 7th month and lasts for seven days.

FEAST OF TABERNACLE

73

# THE MAGI WORSHIP THE KING

There was a clatter in the quiet streets of Bethlehem; the scurry of children, the bustle of older folk hurrying from their houses to see the strangers ride by — Magi, Wise Men from the East, the winged emblem on their garments proclaiming them worshippers of Ahura Mazda, the god of light.

They rode proudly as any king: Caspar, erect and noble in spite of his camel's rolling gait; Melchior, his fine face black as polished ebony, and Balthazar, old now, but serene, his eyes so full of hope and expectation that they seemed to shine with the fire of youth. He stooped as he rode, his thoughts lost in the wonder of the star which had appeared so suddenly on their horizon — a star they had waited for so long and which now seemed to beckon them on.

They had attendants: serious-faced Persians, impish camel boys, dark-skinned with laughing eyes, and baggage which showed they had travelled far.

The little boys of Bethlehem, who ran beside the cavalcade, gazed in wonderment, chattering excitedly, hoping – though they were not beggars — for a sweetmeat or coin to be tossed to them.

The Magi rode on, wondering perhaps at

the simplicity of the place. They had searched for, but had not found, an infant King in Jerusalem — the star had led them here. What a search it had been since that night when the new star flamed in the midnight sky to herald the Birth of a great and mighty King!

Herod, who ruled the Jews, knew of no such Child, but his scribes had said there was such a prophecy, and so they were here in the narrow streets of Bethlehem, where people stood in doorways, at street corners; up the narrow alleys — people who laughed when asked if a Child had been born, for weren't babies being born every day?

As for a *King* — they shrugged. Though they, of all people, should have remembered the prophecy of Micah: "But thou, O Bethlehem, in the land of Judah are by no means least among the rulers of Judah, for from you shall come a Ruler who shall govern My people Israel."

But the prophets had been silent for centuries and only a few rabbis, well-learned in the Scriptures, remembered. And so Christ had come . . . unknown, unrecognised.

There was a small house down the road where Joseph, the young Mother and the Child had lived since "Oh, since the taxing and that was — how long ago?" muttered a man near the inn door." But what did it matter, anyway?"

And now memory jogged their minds as the villagers watched the strangers ride along the road.

"I remember the crowds that flocked here that night," said the innkeeper. "Every nook and cranny was filled to overflowing; we made a lot of money that time . . . "

"My fields were badly trampled," grumbled another, "newly ploughed too. The gipsies took care — they kept to the hillsides — but the city strangers, they had little thought for us."

"I'm glad I let the Nazareth family have the stable," said the innkeeper, suddenly recollecting the incident. "Of course, old Joseph had relations here — he was a Bethlehem man – but even *they* couldn't find shelter for them. You can't turn people away who've paid, but when I said we were full up they didn't grumble or beg. But somehow, as I looked at the Maiden, oh, I don't know . . . but . . . well . . . I let them have the stable — and the Child was born that night. They've stayed in the village ever since, in that little house yonder."

Yes, they had stayed in Bethlehem. Old Joseph made a fair living, they didn't need much, and a skilled carpenter can always get honest work — even if not for a just pay!

The village children flocked to the small house to nurse the Baby or to listen to the Mother who, when work was over, would sit 'like a queen', the Baby on her knee. But that was just children's fanciful talk and they were scolded, for everyone knew that the Mother worked like any other mother.

Queen? Could her Son be a KING?

The people shrugged, angry with the thoughts that were the result of the visit of these strangers. And yet . . . a star *had* shone that night, and gipsies had talked about lights. Shepherds who came to see the young Child said they had seen a host of Angels, that they had come to see Christ the Lord.

It had been a nine days wonder; then the crowds had returned to their own homes and life had flowed on as usual.

Yes, the strangers might try the house . . . but surely they wouldn't find a *King!*

Tongues wagged; folk laughed at the idea of having had a King in their midst all this time.

An old man spoke up. "Everyone who visits the little house," he said slowly, "finds comfort, joy and gladness as they gather round the Mother and Child, and good Joseph, too, when he has time. Some even say that the Child looks at you in a way that makes you ashamed . . . or at peace." He shook his head, as the Magi rode away.

They reached the small house where the young Child was.

Here at last, their search was ended.

They dismounted and, going in, found the Child with Mary His Mother. And they fell down and worshipped Him and, opening their treasures, they offered Him gifts . . . gold, frankincense and myrrh.

# A BIBLE QUIZ

**Can you say whether these statements are RIGHT or WRONG?**

1. The story of the shepherds and the Birth of Christ is found only in St. Luke's Gospel.

2. The story of the Magi is found only in St. Matthew's Gospel.

3. The shepherds heard the news after the Magi had been to see the Child.

4. The shepherds took gifts of beads, a spoon of horn and a lamb.

5. The Magi took gold, frankincense and myrrh.

6. The Magi are called Wise Men and Kings. Which is most correct?

7. The Magi found the Baby in a stable.

8. They worshipped Egyptian gods.

9. They asked Herod, in Jerusalem, where the Child should be born.

10. Herod asked the Magi to return and tell him where they found the Child as he wished to worship a new king. Was this true?

11. The Magi obeyed Herod, returned to tell him that they had found the Baby in Bethlehem.

12. In England and many other countries Christmas is kept on 25th December. What is commemorated at Epiphany, 6th January?

*Answers on page 126*

# A BIBLE LEGEND

There is a legend that near the Bethlehem house grew a great oak tree, an olive and a small fir tree. The two big trees began to boast: "I," said the oak, "spread my branches for shade when the Mother puts the Baby in His cradle outside."

"I," said the olive, "let my fruit drop so that the Mother may have oil for the Child."

"I can do nothing," sighed the little fir. "My prickly branches would hurt Him. My cones are too hard for His fingers. What can I give Him?"

"Nothing!" mocked the two trees.

But a passing Angel heard the conversation. He dropped a star on the little fir tree. It twinkled and sparkled so much that the Baby in the cradle clapped His hands for joy.

# SPICES OF THE BIBLE

**ALOES.** A succulent plant, its thick fleshy leaves forming a rosette just above the roots. The flowers are bright vermillion, shading to clear yellow. Its blue-grey leaves contain *aloin*, a substance which can be dissolved in water and added to incense and used for purifying the bodies of the departed. The condensed juice is also a purgative and was known to the ancients. The leaves, when pressed, give a bright purple juice.

Aloes

Rue          Spices

**RUE** is a garden herb mentioned only once in the Bible. It was used as a disinfectant and was scattered in courts of justice to protect the officials from disease and the terrible smells. It is useful in medicine as well as in cookery.

**SPICES.** They were used for the holy incense offered in the Temple. A ball of cotton is passed over the plant to collect the accumulated lumps of gum.

**MYRRH** is the gum resin of a big bush or tree. The trunk is large and bears many knotted branches whose outer bark is thin and papery. Small leaves grow on the wood in clusters. The bark is pierced and a thick white gum appears. It hardens and turns a reddish colour when exposed to the air.

It has been collected and sold as a spice and medicine from earliest times.

In Bible days the tree grew along the coast of the Red Sea. The resin was collected and conveyed to the east by merchants on camels. Nicodemus brought a hundred pounds (in weight) to be placed in the linen cloths which wrapped the Body of Jesus when He was buried in the Tomb, (S. John 19.39,40).

Myrrh

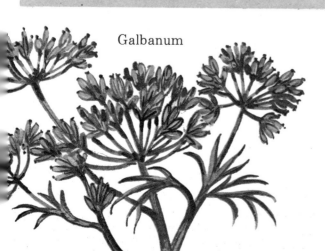

Galbanum

**GALBANUM.** This was another spice mixed with incense which was burned on the altar in the Holy Place. It has a fetid, yellowish gum resin containing a substance called *umbelliferone*. In Bible days it was imported. When it is ripe the young stem is cut a few inches above the ground and a milky juice flows out. It hardens quickly. When burned, its odour is pungent but pleasant.

79

# FOODS OF THE BIBLE

You will all have eaten a walnut, perhaps in cake or toffee or, at Christmas, you will have had the kernals on their own; or have you tried pickled walnuts?

These green nuts for pickling are available in July from a greengrocer. They are pricked all over (and they dye your fingers brown!); put on a dish; covered with salt and placed in the sunshine to become brown. The brine is drained off and the nuts are bottled in spiced vinegar.

A heavy rind covers the kernal and if this is soaked in boiling water it produces a rich brown dye.

The nut has male and female catkins (flowers) on the same bush. They appear in February before the leaves unfold.

There were walnut trees in Solomon's gardens, handsome trees which gave shade in that hot land. The Greeks called it the 'Persian Tree' and held their feasts under the branches.

In heathen mythology it was dedicated to the god Jove.

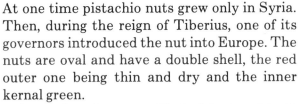

At one time pistachio nuts grew only in Syria. Then, during the reign of Tiberius, one of its governors introduced the nut into Europe. The nuts are oval and have a double shell, the red outer one being thin and dry and the inner kernal green.

Some chocolates are filled with pistachio. It is like green marzipan.

A favourite sweetmeat was made by mixing honey, nuts, dates and gum arabic into cakes.

Spices were used by all but the very poor.

Lentils, beans, garlic, leeks, olives and onions were much enjoyed. Dates, pomegranates, melons and figs were great favourites.

**FIGS** were not usually cultivated in groves, but singly, or in groups. They grew well near dwellings and could reach a height of thirty feet, giving shade – always welcome in a hot land. The first fruit buds appear in February or March, but much of the fruit fails to mature. Those which do are called 'early figs' and they have a fine flavour. The chief crop comes in August or September; they are deep purple, green, whitish or nearly black. They are eaten fresh or dried into cakes. The sort we eat in Britain are really small 'cakes of figs'. Sometimes we see them packed into wooden boxes. Usually there is a dried fig leaf on top of the 'cake'. In the East the leaves are still sewn together to make wrappings for fresh fruit for market.

The Egyptians considered the fig to be the Tree of Life and believed that one of their godesses presented figs to mortals who were thought worthy of eternal life!

**BETHPHAGE** (House of Unripe Figs) where Jesus sent His disciples to get the ass on which He made His triumphal entry into Jerusalem, was near Bethany on the Mount of Olives. Its exact site is unknown. It was famous for the fruit.

**SYCOMORE FIG** (or mulberry fig), which was cultivated by the prophet Amos, was evergreen. The small fruits had to be pricked to speed ripening. The wood of this tree was prized more than the fruit. Zacchaeus climbed such a tree in an attempt to catch a glimpse of Jesus, Who called to him to come down as He wished to dine with him. This was a great honour for a tax gatherer. They were hated because of their trade, tax collectors often forcing unjust dues from the people.

**SALT** was used in vast quantities. It was obtained from the Mediterranean and Dead Seas and evaporated in pans. There were, also, salt mines. It was used for preserving dried fish, olives and certain vegetables.

Salt has always been a sign of friendship. To this day Arabs say: "There is salt between us", meaning that a bond has been forged by the eating of salt. Bedouins believe that a new born baby should be rubbed with salt.

**SALARY** was, at first, the allowance made to a Roman soldier for the purchase of salt. Syria taxed it in order to raise money for her dues to Rome.

# JESUS IS TAKEN TO THE TEMPLE

Mary held the Baby in her arms, but her eyes gazed beyond. "Son of the Most High," she marvelled, "yet *my* Son!"

For a few years she would teach Him, tell Him very simply how the Angel had come, how the whole sky was aflame with the glory of the Angels on the night of His Birth; how Magi had come . . .

Yes, Magi had come. They had brought rich gifts, which lay in the great chest of cedar wood which Joseph had made. Cedar wood, like that in the Temple, sweet smelling, rich in colour but simple in design.

Later Joseph would teach the Child. Later still He would go to the village school where the old rabbi mumbled the Scriptures.

She laughed gently. What was she doing, thinking of school and the Baby but forty days old!

She rose and went into the workshop. She liked the curled wood shavings, the pleasant smell. She liked to watch Joseph at work.

He paused and smiled as she entered, then his saw moved to and fro, to and fro. His thoughts were not unlike Mary's; what a joy it would be to tell the Child the mysteries of His Birth.

But he wouldn't speak of the cruel wagging tongues . . . though he might confess how he had thought of breaking the betrothal, privately, to spare her what pain he might, remembering his tortured thoughts until a solution was found in a dream: "Fear not to take unto you Mary, your wife, for that which is born of her is of the Holy Ghost . . . she shall bring forth a Son and you shall call His Name Jesus."

He looked at Mary, met her gentle loving gaze and felt at peace.

He wiped his tools on an oily rag, put them away carefully and made ready for the Temple. He tied a coin in a corner of his mantle.

"It is a pity we cannot offer a lamb and a dove," he said, "but the Temple charges are so high. Two doves must serve."

Mary nodded. She would weave a new cloak for Joseph, his old one was so shabby. Someday she would weave the Child a fine robe, without seam, and dyed a rich colour.

As they walked along the road children ran to greet them; Mary smiled and people smiled back at her joy.

The Court of the Gentiles was very crowded, but at last their Roman money was exchanged and two doves bought. Then they went into the Court of the Women where great, trumpet-shaped chests stood for offerings. It was all so beautiful, so right that the Child should be here.

Old Simeon the priest watched them coming, the light glinting on the jewels of his vesture, his eyes shining with joy as the little family drew near. This was the moment he had waited for – the great moment of his life – for here came the Messiah, the Chosen One!

He hurried to take the Child and, filled with prophetic wonder cried: "Lord, now lettest Thou Thy servant depart in peace according to Thy word, for mine eyes have seen Thy salvation, which Thou hast prepared for all peoples; a Light to lighten the Gentiles and to be the glory of Thy people Israel."

He blessed Mary and Joseph and turned to Mary and said: "Behold, this Child is set for the falling and rising up of many in Israel; for a sign which shall be spoken against . . ." he hesitated, distressed, loath to say what must be said. "Yes, and a sword shall pierce through your own soul also that the thoughts of many hearts may be revealed."

Mary looked at the Babe with wondering eyes, but before she could speak, old Anna the prophetess, came from the shadows cast by the great columns of the Temple – old Anna who spent her days in prayer, fasting and worship.

Her face was like wrinkled parchment but her eyes were bright with happiness.

She stood beside Simeon and gazed at the Infant.

"O, give thanks unto the Lord," she cried, "for now I behold the redemption of Israel."

Simeon looked at her. She, too, recognised the Promised One.

He gave the Baby back to the young Mother . . . a sword should pierce through her soul, he had said.

But Mary was smiling as she looked at her Baby. Come pain, come sorrow, all suffering was lost in present joy. Jesus was in her arms. Nothing else mattered.

They had fulfilled the Law. They saw the old priest and prophetess standing in rapt wonder, then they turned and went home.

# NATIONAL HEALTH

As long ago as 2100 B.C. in Mesopotamia the legal code of Hammurabi fixed the amount of doctors' fees and imposed penalties on surgeons who "carelessly performed operations"!

No one knows how many physicians and surgeons there were in comparison with the population, and most people depended on traditional family cures. Egypt gained knowledge from Mesopotamia and this passed on to Greece, but a great deal of magic was mixed with that knowledge.

It is to the great Greek doctor Hippocrates that we owe the famous oath which binds doctors today when they swear to put the life and welfare of the patient above all else.

There must have been some anodyne, for drugs used to alleviate pain such as at the crucifixions when gall, mixed with vinegar, was offered to the condemned. Our Lord refused this, although later He accepted a drink which was not mixed with pain killer.

*(Matthew 27, Verse 34 and 48)*

There was a definite school of medicine at Alexandria.

A stamp for printing on a box was discovered which ran: "Saffron ointment for scars and discharges prepared by Junius Taurus after the prescription of Poccius". Another inscription says: "The anodyne of Q. Junius Taurus for every kind of defective eyesight".

The Law of Moses made it quite clear that 1st century Jews had a number of regulations regarding hygiene. The rabbis were keen observers of the law of health, and were often in advance of mid 19th century practice! They ordered that every town should have at least a physician who understood surgery and these were supposed to hold a licence from the rabbi.

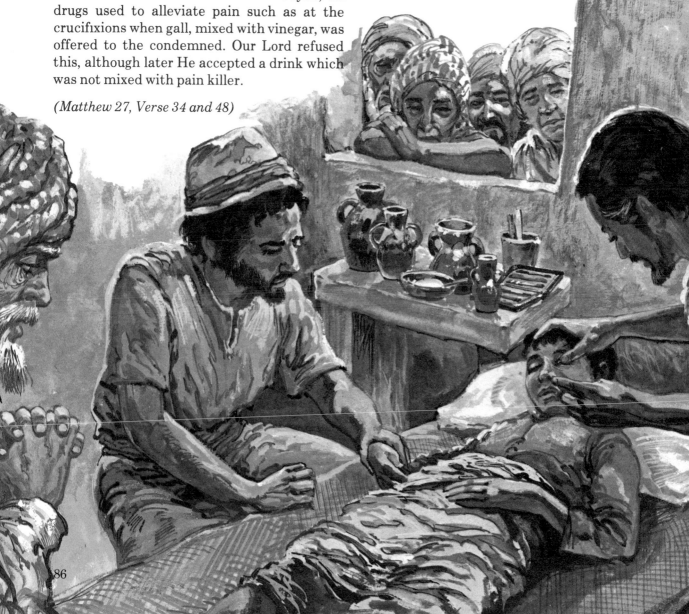

**GALL**

Alas, not all doctors were true to their vows, and many put politics first and gained a bad name for their colleagues.

There was always a physician among the Temple officials, for the priests had to perform their religious duties barefoot, which led to occupational diseases.

Prescriptions were chiefly herbal. The uses of cold water compresses and baths were known.

Dental treatment was known as early as 3700 B.C. Tooth stopping was found in mummies, and false teeth were used. These were made from the teeth of dead people and animals.

Toothpaste was in vogue in the 1st century A.D. Calcined bones and powdered oyster shell were mixed into a paste with honey. Myrhh, nitre and hartshorn were ingredients, not only to whiten the teeth but to harden the gums and, possibly, for toothache.

## THINGS TO DO

1. See how many 'traditional' remedies Mother or Grandma can give you, perhaps for coughs and colds.

Here is one for a hacking cough and some types of sore throat: Boil a tablespoonful of linseed in two cupfuls of water. Drain through a sieve. Add the juice of one lemon and some crushed 'spanish' (hard, black licquorice, obtainable at most chemists). Sweeten with honey.

2. If you have an old established family chemist ask if he has a very ancient 'tooth extractor' – it was chemists who, originally, pulled out teeth!

# HAIR FASHIONS

Josephus, who lived shortly after Jesus, but before the Temple at Jerusalem was destroyed, said that young men of his day sprinkled their hair with powdered gold dust to make it shine!

Baldness was a disgrace and well-to-do Jews allowed their hair to grow shoulder length. If a Jew made a vow to the Lord they sometimes did not cut their hair while this vow lasted. Then it was cut off and presented for a sacrifice.

In the Jewish Book called the Mishna the people were forbidden to plait their hair on the Sabbath, so we know that some wore it in this style.

If they were going to a banquet they annointed their heads with oil and sometimes with perfume.

A strange custom of certain tribes in Arabia was to cut off the hair of their vanquished enemy as an act of vengeance, which was much better than cutting off their heads. Then the chin was shaved for further humiliation.

A Hebrew would bow to a man with white hair as a token of reverence for old age.

Hebrew women wore their hair bound and veiled.

Egyptians thought cleanliness, as well as coolness, was important, and they wore their hair short or even shaved. For special occasions they wore wigs.

**DO YOU KNOW** that some *queens* wore *beards*? They were held in position with a strap. HATSHAPAUT (1505–1482 B.C.) was such a queen! In Cairo Museum there is a famous sandstone shrine founded by this queen.

Samuel tells us that one of King Saul's sons "neither dressed his feet, nor trimmed his beard nor even washed his clothes!"

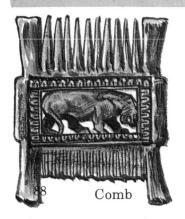

Comb

# MONEY

You can do a lot of things with money, but can you imagine your fathers paying for something with lumps of gold?

We talk about "not having two coins to rub against each other", and that means we are very 'hard up'.

Yet Solomon, who was the richest man of his time, could have said that *he* hadn't two coins to rub together, even though he had an income of 666 weighed talents, besides that which came from traders and others, (1. Kings.ch.10.14).

He ruled from 973 B.C. to 933 B.C. but the first coin did not appear in trade until a King of Lydia invented it in the 7th Century B.C. This was shortly before the time of King Croesus *What* saying do you know about *him*?

Cyrus, the Persian, conquered Croesus and carried away the coined money (546 B.C.) and Darius, his successor, sent minted coins throughout the Persian-Babylonian world of trade.

Didrachma. Tyre A.D. 14

Shekel 140 B.C. – A.D. 66

**DO YOU KNOW** that references to money in the Old Testament even confuse students of the Bible? You see, the talent and shekel, which later denoted minted coins, were, at first, units of weight.

The word *shekel* comes from the Hebrew sháqal (to weigh).

One of the talents which came into use equalled 6,000 denarii, or drachmas.

The denarius (singular) was the most convenient coin in the time of Christ for it was equivalent to a labourer's daily wage.

## WEIGHTS OF OLDEN BIBLE DAYS.

1 homer = 10 ephahs = 30 seáhs = 180 kabs = 720 logs = 10 bushels.

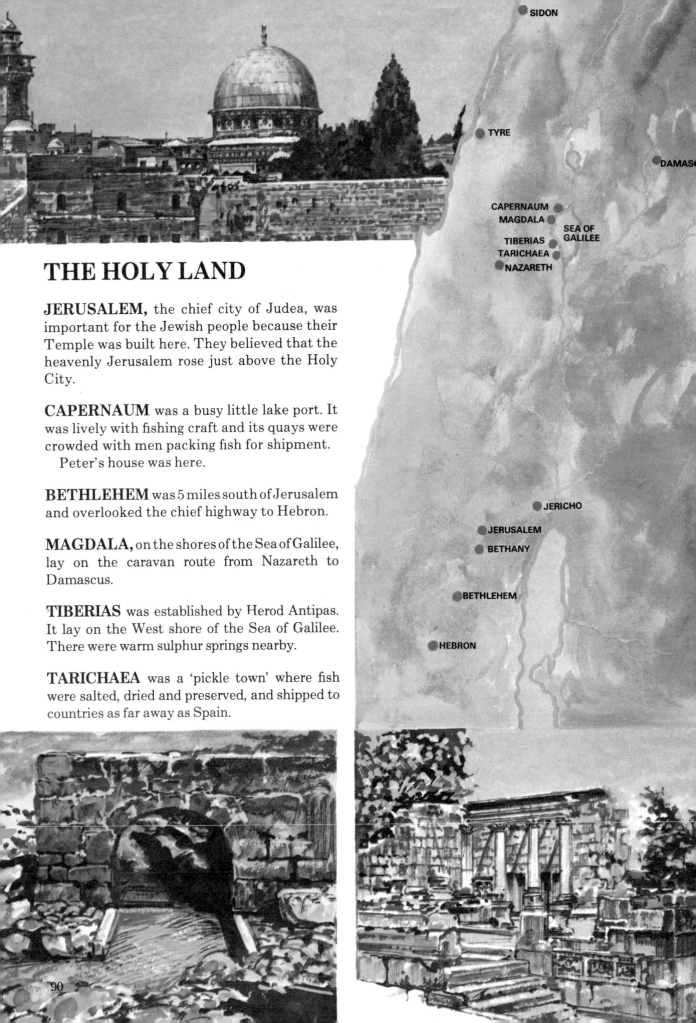

# THE HOLY LAND

**JERUSALEM,** the chief city of Judea, was important for the Jewish people because their Temple was built here. They believed that the heavenly Jerusalem rose just above the Holy City.

**CAPERNAUM** was a busy little lake port. It was lively with fishing craft and its quays were crowded with men packing fish for shipment.
     Peter's house was here.

**BETHLEHEM** was 5 miles south of Jerusalem and overlooked the chief highway to Hebron.

**MAGDALA,** on the shores of the Sea of Galilee, lay on the caravan route from Nazareth to Damascus.

**TIBERIAS** was established by Herod Antipas. It lay on the West shore of the Sea of Galilee. There were warm sulphur springs nearby.

**TARICHAEA** was a 'pickle town' where fish were salted, dried and preserved, and shipped to countries as far away as Spain.

SIDON

TYRE

DAMAS

CAPERNAUM
MAGDALA
TIBERIAS
TARICHAEA
NAZARETH
SEA OF GALILEE

JERICHO
JERUSALEM
BETHANY
BETHLEHEM
HEBRON

# MAP QUIZ

1. A certain man went down to Jer . . . . . . from Jer . . . . and fell among thieves.

2. Jesus went to a wedding at . . . . of Galilee.

3. Jesus was born in . . . . . . . .

4. Many of the Apostles, who were fishermen, plied their trade on the Sea of . . . . . . .

5. The Great Sea is now called the M . . . . . . . . . . . Sea.

6. The river running from top to bottom of the map is the . . . . . .

7. J . . . . . . . was the chief city of Palestine.

8. The T . . . . . was there and every Jew tried to visit this house of God.

9. The Virgin Mary lived in N . . . . . . .

10. C . . . . . . . by the Sea of Galilee, where Jesus spent much of His public ministry.

11. Mary, Martha and Lazarus, friends of Jesus, lived in . . . . . . .

12. Golgotha, where Our Lord was crucified was just outside the Holy C . . . (J . . . . . . . . )

*Answers on page 126*

## INTERESTING ITEMS

The Temple at Jerusalem was one of the great wonders of the world. The roof of the Sanctuary – the Holy Place and Holy of Holies – was covered with gold. Spikes were fixed in it to prevent birds from alighting there and soiling it.

In the Holy Place was a table and a lamp-stand (or candlestick) of gold. The altar of incense was overlaid with pure gold. A veil hung across the opening into the Holy of Holies, which was dark and quite empty, the Ark having been lost. The High Priest might enter once in the year, on the Day of Atonement.

# THE BOY IN THE TEMPLE

Every Jewish boy looked forward to his thirteenth year, when he would go to the synagogue to be recognised as a 'son of the Law'; to incur a man's responsibilities; to be admitted to the full privileges of his religion, and to go to Jerusalem for the Passover.

It was a journey to be looked forward to with wonder. It was fun, too; you met so many people from so many different places; you exchanged talk; perhaps had to stifle laughter as you struggled towards friendship with one whose dialect was so different from your own that it seemed more like a foreign language.

Travelling from Nazareth in the north you would pass many exciting places, places you had heard so much about but had never seen . . . wonderful shrines, and though many of them were in ruins, imagination would restore some of them to their ancient glory.

So said one boy to another as the day for departure drew near.

This year Jesus was joining the eager crowds.

The caravan, as the long stream of people was called, grew bigger and bigger at each crossroads. Some people travelled in grand style, some on asses, many on foot.

One night they might rest at Shunem and hear stories of Elisha, and a feeling of awe would come upon them as they realised that here, where they trod, had lived their great prophet. They might pass Bethel and remember that here Jacob saw his 'ladder' of angels, host upon host, from earth to the skies, and heard God's voice.

On . . . on . . . and problems would be discussed and great matters talked over and the Boy's eyes would shine as He entered into the debates.

ON . . . on . . . until at last Jerusalem was sighted, and with fervent zeal they lifted up their voices in the processional psalms: "I was glad when they said unto me, let us go into the House of the Lord."

What were the thoughts of Jesus as He glimpsed the shining, dazzling beauty before Him, heard wave after wave of song, as is the way when people sing in procession?

On . . . on . . . through the Damascus Gate – and now they were really in the Holy City! Past the pillars of the Temple precincts, through the crowded, noisy Court of the Gentiles, where a man must change his foreign money for Temple coinage before he could buy a sacrificial lamb – and pay five times its worth; up the twelve great steps to the sacred fence, through the shining brass gateway, up five more steps, through the Court of the Women, fifteen steps to the Court of Israel where a glimpse might be caught of the edifice which hid the Holy of Holies.

It was a day to be remembered, closing with the great Feast of the Passover, when the youngest boy said to the oldest man present: "What mean ye by this service?" And the old story was retold and at last the lamb was eaten.

The days that followed must have been full. Often Jesus must have longed to return to the Temple to wonder about the new consciousness which was dawning upon Him – *Christ* consciousness.

The bustle of departure came too soon. Did the Boy run off to the Temple for a last, quick talk with His Father, intending to catch up with the caravan?

Perhaps the joy of being in His Father's House made Him lose all count of time, and soon He was on the terrace where, at festival times, great rabbis and doctors of the Law, such as Gamaliel and Nicodemus, gathered to teach.

Anyone might go there, and now Jesus was among them, asking and answering questions with such wisdom that the teachers were astonished at His understanding.

Mary and Joseph did not miss Him until the long caravan halted later in the evening, when families gathered their young together for a meal and prayers.

But Jesus did not come.

There were no welcoming shouts; no hurrying footsteps.

Anxiously Mary and Joseph went from group to group: "Have you seen Jesus?"

Always the answer was the same:

So they hurried back to Jerusalem to search until there was only one likely place left. So they went to the Temple . . . and there He was!

"Oh son, son, why did you do this to us? We have looked everywhere for you," cried Mary, hurrying to Him.

He looked at His Mother, gently, and lovingly but with wonderment as He replied: "But didn't you know that I must be about My Father's business?"

Did He pat her arm and smile at her as at once He went with them – out of His Father's House?

"And He went down with them and they came to Nazareth and He was subject unto them . . . but His Mother kept all these things in her heart . . . and Jesus daily increased in stature and found favour with God and man."

# WHO?

**Who said :**

1. Hail, O favoured one, the Lord is with you.

2. Behold the handmaid of the Lord, be it unto me according to Thy word.

3. Glory to God in the highest and on earth peace to men of good will.

4. Lord, now lettest Thou Thy servant depart in peace, for mine eyes have seen Thy salvation.

5. Render unto Caesar the things that are Caesar's and to God the things that are God's.

6. If You are the Son of God command this stone to become bread.

7. Judge not and you shall not be judged.

8. I see no fault in this just Man.

9. Father, forgive them for they know not what they do.

10. Woman behold your son; behold your mother.

11. They have taken away my Lord and I do not know where they have laid Him.

12. Receive the Holy Spirit; if you forgive the sins of any, they are forgiven; if you retain the sins of any, they are retained.

If you can say to WHOM the words were said, give yourself double marks.

*Answers on page 126*

# MAKE A LILY OF THE FIELD

The flowers referred to in the Bible as lilies of the field were really ANEMONES. You CAN MAKE ONE like this.

**Materials:** Tissue paper – scarlet, purple, cream; a little black and green; handful of cotton wool; very fine wire; a little strong glue; pencil; scissors; paper for patterns.

**Method.** Pin the patterns on the tissue paper as required and cut 1 each: petal strip (Fig. 1) scarlet; stamens (fringe as in Fig. 2) circle for centre (2″ diameter) black; (3A) frill (Fig. 5) and stem strip (5″ x ½″) green.

Make a cotton wool ball, elongated into cone shape (Fig. 3). Place centrally on the black circle (Fig. 3A) and twist firmly. Wrap the stamen strip round the 'cone' close to the ball (2B); add a dab of glue and follow on with the scarlet petal strip, (1A), pleating as you wrap. Finish with another dab of glue. Tie these firmly with a 6″ piece of wire (Fig. 4) leaving the long end for the stalk.

Glue one end of the stalk strip, attach just below the petals to cover the wire wrap, and bring it round and down the stalk to the end, where you finish off with a dab of glue. Cut the green sepals (Fig. 5) pierce with the stalk and slide it upwards to within one inch of the flower base. Open out the petals for a natural look.

Repeat, using other colours, to make a bunch of 'lilies of the field', varying the position of the 'frill' for variety.

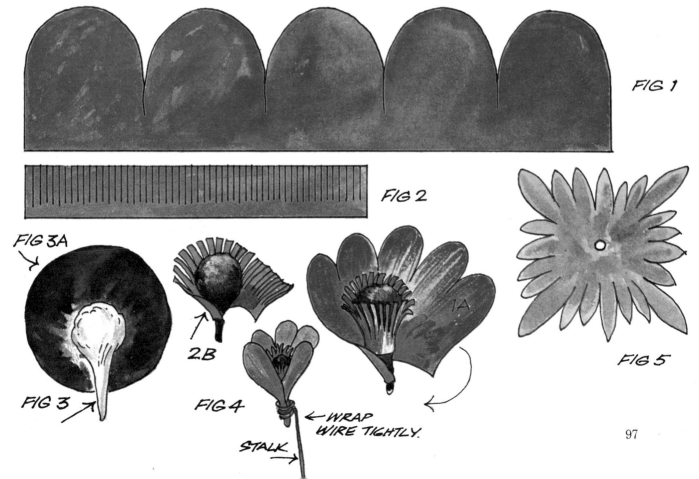

FIG 1

FIG 2

FIG 3A

2B

FIG 3

FIG 4

WRAP WIRE TIGHTLY.

STALK

1A

FIG 5

# THE VOICE OF THE TEMPTER

Power, position, popularity, these were within reach ... but Christ rejected them ... and *triumphed*.

The road from Jerusalem to Jericho descends thousands of feet through almost trackless desert. This is a most desolate wilderness, a place of deep ravines, overhanging cliffs and sulphurous rocks of grotesque shapes. Wild beasts roam; the heat is intense. It is a place to dread, to avoid.

Yet Jesus came here to spend those forty days of solitude, fasting and prayer, in retreat from the world before He took up His public ministry.

He had been baptised by John, had seen the heavens open as the Holy Spirit descended upon Him. He had heard His Father's Voice clearly: "This is My beloved Son in whom I am well pleased."

After the glory – the wilderness.

How often the desire for food and water, for familiar scenes, must have assailed Him. There is no record of those days spent alone. Only later, we suppose, did He talk to His Apostles, the Twelve He was soon to choose. Did He tell them the final drama, perhaps so that others might be comforted to know that the sinless One was tempted, "like as we are", and triumphed?

Now it was time to return to the world, suffering all the pangs of starvation and weariness.

It was then that the devil came. Perhaps Jesus, seeking for wild honey or berries to sustain Himself for the homeward journey, picked up one of the flat stones, so like, in shape and colour, the bread baked at home. Bread! He had often watched it being made, and there came to mind the fragrance of newly-baked loaves – torment to a hungry man.

He turned the stone over in His hand.

"So like bread," whispered Satan, softly. "Bread! Freshly baked bread. If you are the Son of God command these stones to be turned into bread that You may eat."

We can almost hear the crash of stone against stone as He flung it from Him and turned to the tempter.

Loudly He said: "Man shall not live by bread alone but by every word of God." He had learned those words as a Child.

Satan watched the exhausted figure toil slowly up the seemingly endless steeps.

Across the wilderness shone now the white houses of Jerusalem; the shining pinnacles of the Temple towering against the sky.

*"And the devil set Jesus on the pinnacle of the Temple".*

Below were the vast courts, open to the sky . . . great pillars, tiled floors of rare beauty; priests in vestments blazoned with precious jewels were at worship in His Father's House.

"Jerusalem," whispered Satan, "the Temple where *You* should reign. If You *are* the Son of God, cast Yourself down before the vast worshipping crowds. Let priests and people see the glory of the Messiah. Is it not written: "He shall give His angels charge over You lest You dash Your foot against a stone?" Cast Yourself down; be acclaimed Messiah. . ." the voice rose, thundering, tormenting. . . "*If* You are God. . . . if. . . . *if*. . . ."

Jesus turned and answered quotation with quotation: "It is also written: "You shall not tempt the Lord your God.'

Did He sink to the ground in utter exhaustion, suffering physically from the struggle?

Did the devil look down at Him scornfully, thinking the battle won as he said: "Below You is the Holy City, gateway to the world. Behold, kingdom upon kingdom stretched out before You . . . so fair . . . so glorious. All power shall be Yours if You will kneel to me. Sink just a little lower to the ground . . . a single movement in Your exhaustion, and I will give You the whole world. Kneel, where none may see You. Take the easy way . . . a brief gesture – then rise, King of the world. Kneel . . . *kneel* . . ."

Jesus looked at the glories spread before Him in an instant of time.

Then He stood up and His voice was terrible.

"Get you behind Me, Satan, for it is written: You shall worship the Lord your God and Him only shall you serve."

Then the devil left Him for a season.

*(Read the two versions in St. Matthew, chapter 4 1-12, and St. Luke, chapter 4 1-13)*

# ODDS AND ENDS

The cash drawer of a Jerusalem merchant in the New Testament times might have contained:

Some old Persian silver *siglos* or gold *darics* (equal to one English sovereign) brought back to Jerusalem by returning captives and still in circulation.

Small bronze and silver coins struck by the Maccabean John Hyrcanus.

Various minted coins from Phoenician mints at Tyre and Sidon, especially shekels and tetradrachmas.

Greek gold and silver coins, gold *staters* and others.

Roman coins, the silver denarius (mentioned at least sixteen times in the New Testament (R.S.V.)

Egyptian coins.

In Bible times sandals were worn outside, but in the tent or house, the feet were bare. This is why it was always polite to offer water and towels to a guest for the washing of feet.

The head dress of today's tent dweller is so well planned as a protection against heat or cold wind that it is probably the same as that worn in Bible days.

Josephus Flavius was a Jewish historian born in Jerusalem A.D. 37 or 38. He died in Rome A.D. 100. He is not mentioned in the Bible but he has helped towards an understanding of the Scriptures and a better idea of the Jewish background of Christian history than any other writer. He describes the Temple which was not then destroyed.

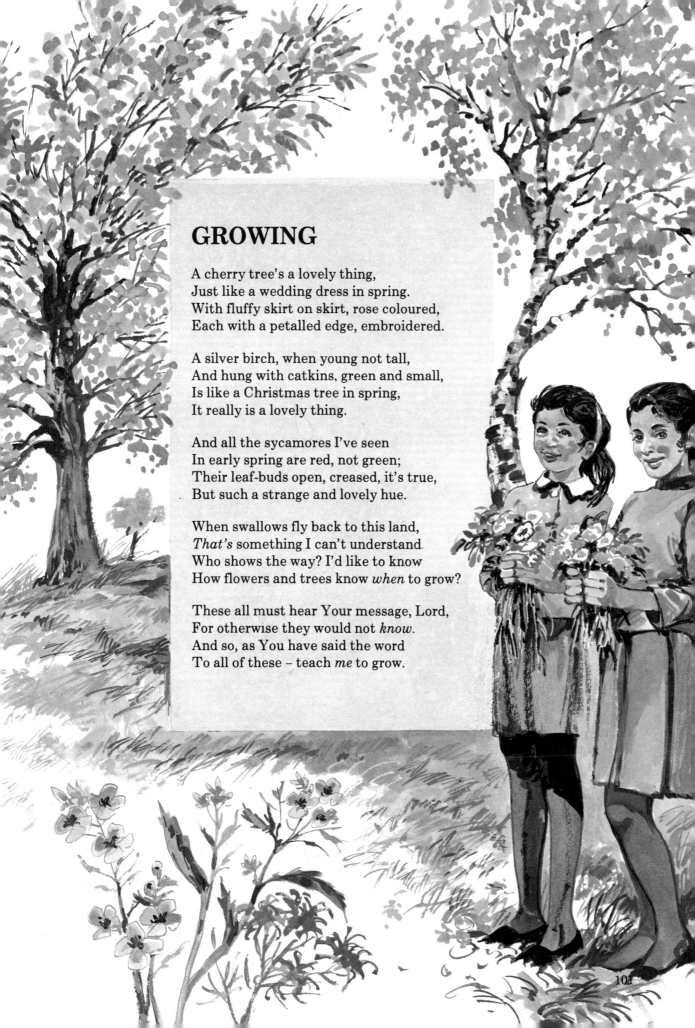

# GROWING

A cherry tree's a lovely thing,
Just like a wedding dress in spring.
With fluffy skirt on skirt, rose coloured,
Each with a petalled edge, embroidered.

A silver birch, when young not tall,
And hung with catkins, green and small,
Is like a Christmas tree in spring,
It really is a lovely thing.

And all the sycamores I've seen
In early spring are red, not green;
Their leaf-buds open, creased, it's true,
But such a strange and lovely hue.

When swallows fly back to this land,
*That's* something I can't understand.
Who shows the way? I'd like to know
How flowers and trees know *when* to grow?

These all must hear Your message, Lord,
For otherwise they would not *know*.
And so, as You have said the word
To all of these – teach *me* to grow.

# THE PROMISED ONE

Jesus Christ returned from the wilderness refreshed by angels, the shining light of purpose in His eyes. As he walked, His stride was sure, alert.

He glanced this way and that, but His thoughts were on His cousin John, nicknamed 'the Baptist'. John had prepared the way for Him faithfully, fervently, sternly, saying: "He who comes after me is mightier than I. He shall baptise you with the Holy Ghost and with fire. He shall cleanse His threshing floor... gather the wheat into His garner . . . and the chaff into everlasting fire."

He was over there, surrounded by a mixed crowd.

Jesus looked across from the slope on which He now halted, picking out the faces He had come to know. That young man, dark-haired, clean-shaven, eager-eyed, was John, son of Zebedee; yes, and Andrew, son of Jonas.

Suddenly the Baptist looked up, saw Jesus standing there in the sunshine which lit up the face of the Son of God.

"Behold the Lamb of God who takes away the sins of the world," he cried, so loudly that the crowd turned, gazed, and wondered.

"It's Jesus," exclaimed young John.

"You must follow *Him*, now," said the Baptist. "I am not worthy even to unfasten His shoe."

The young John and Andrew looked at the Man proclaimed 'Lamb of God'. Then they turned and left the Baptist, whom they had followed for so long, to hasten after Jesus who was walking away.

"Hurry," urged John, "or we shall lose sight of Him."

Their hearts thudded, their feet refused to hasten, or so it seemed, in their anxiety to catch up. Suddenly Jesus turned.

"What do you want? Whom do you seek?" He asked.

John didn't answer. An answer didn't seem important – all that mattered was that they should see Jesus again. So he asked: "Master, where do You live?"

Jesus smiled. "Come with Me and I will show you," He replied.

As they walked, John related how the Baptist had taught of the One who should come – the Messiah; how He had said "Behold the Lamb of God".

"– so we followed," said Andrew.

Outside the town, Jesus stopped before a rough tent.

"This is My dwelling," He said. "Come in – make yourselves comfortable. Ask Me all the questions I see you are longing to ask."

It was about four o'clock, and all that evening they talked, talked, talked. Perhaps the two young men did most of the questioning for they must be *sure* that here was the Messiah, the Promised One of Israel.

The Baptist had prepared them, preaching repentance for the remission of sins, telling them of the salvation of God. But now they were amazed. Had they expected a great king? Yet this peasant Man had an air of authority. He answered as one who understood, and told them something of His plans.

We can imagine a lamp being lit, food being offered and enjoyed, slowly, pleasurably, because they were with Him. The tent would grow warm and smoky with the guttering flame. Perhaps they would sit outside – and talk, talk, talk; the noise about them – rowdy shouts and laughter – passing unnoticed, for the Messiah was there!

Walking home that night, absorbed and exultant, knowing that they were to meet the Teacher again, did they talk it all over, their feet making little sound on the cobbled streets, their voices rising with excitement as they recalled all that had been discussed?

Andrew was eager to find his brother Peter, but he must wait until morning.

He was up early, when the world was cool and the water of the lake veiled in a curtain of mist, dispersing now as the sun came up.

Peter was bending over the nets, big, impetuous Peter!

"Hey," shouted Andrew, "you don't know whom I've seen – I've seen the Messiah – and talked with Him. Come with me."

Peter dropped his nets. He must work harder later on. He followed Andrew, listening as his brother poured out the great news. Then tongues were stilled as they saw Jesus.

"So you are Peter?" asked Jesus. "I shall call you Cephas, a *rock*."

Peter looked at the Man before him. He was smiling – yet He was quite serious . . . . and Peter could have knelt in gratitude. Not *clumsy* Peter, but a *rock* . . . a rock to withstand storm and tempest.

"No one ever called me a rock," he whispered.

"You *are* a rock – or shall be," said the Teacher.

There was little time for more. Peter must be back at the nets, but Andrew was satisfied.

The little band of followers was growing.

Jesus smiled as He watched them walk away. They would be back – ready to learn all that He had in mind for them.

His plan was taking shape. . . .

# SOME PRAYERS

I am sure you all know the Prayer Jesus Christ told His followers to say:

OUR FATHER
Who art in heaven;
Hallowed be Thy Name;
Thy Kingdom come;
Thy Will be done on earth
As it is in Heaven.
Give us this day our daily bread
And forgive us our trespasses
As we forgive those who trespass against us;
And lead us not into temptation,
But deliver us from evil,
AMEN.

Sometimes you will find these words added: For Thine is the kingdom, the Power and the Glory, for ever and ever, Amen.

It is called *The Doxology* and was not included when Jesus said the words.

Defend me, O Lord, with your heavenly grace, that I may continue Yours for ever; and daily increase in Your Holy Spirit more and more, until I come to Your everlasting Kingdom. Amen.

At Night, an extra prayer:
The grace of our Lord Jesus Christ and the love of God and the fellowship of the Holy Spirit be with us all evermore. Amen.

# THE TWELVE APOSTLES

At first the Bible calls 'The Twelve' *disciples*, but later they were called Apostles, if one referred to the twelve men specially chosen by Jesus personally. Others who followed Him are disciples.

This is the list given in St. Matthew:

Simon, who is called Peter, and Andrew, his brother; James, the son of Zebedee, and John, his brother; Philip and Bartholomew; Thomas, and Matthew the publican (*tax collector*); James, the son of Alphaeus, and Thaddeus; Simon the Canaanite, and Judas Iscariot, who also betrayed Him.

St. John is known as the 'beloved disciple'. He was probably in his twenties at the time of the Crucifixion. Our Lord gave His Mother into John's care.

St. Peter is thought of as a big, bluff fisherman, generous and loving but apt 'to put his foot into it', as we should say; but he was always sorry afterwards. He was in the courtyard when Jesus was being tried and three times he denied any knowledge of his Master. Then the cock crew and Peter remembered that Jesus had warned him: "Before the cock crows twice thou shalt deny me thrice". Then Peter went out and wept bitterly. He is said to have been crucified upside down.

Thomas Didymus (twin) is remembered for his doubting. He was absent from the group that first Sunday after the Crucifixion, and he refused to believe that the others had seen Jesus in the Upper Room. He said he would not believe unless he could put his finger into the print of the nails and thrust his hand into His side. A week later Jesus came to them again. "My Lord and my God!" cried Thomas. Jesus told him to touch the nail prints and the wound and not to be faithless, but to believe.

St. Matthew was a tax gatherer when Jesus called him to become a follower. This trade was hated by the people.

Can you discover anything about the lesser known Apostles? Ask at school, at Sunday school or at Church.

# LOCUSTS

## (a) Locusts

The locust is the fruit of the carob tree. In the east it is believed that this is what St. John the Baptist ate in the wilderness. The tree is evergreen and very beautiful when in early spring it bears clusters of small pea-shaped blossoms. Bean-like fruits follow. They are rather like English 'broad beans' filled with mucilage that protects the seeds. In the East it is dried as food for man and cattle. It is obtainable at some Health Food shops.

DO YOU KNOW – the carob seed is said to have been the ancient weight used by goldsmiths and from the word we get 'carat' the weight still used.

## (b) Locusts (Insect)

The Hebrew Law allowed locusts to be eaten, and even today the Bedouins and others eat them with unleavened bread and oil. They are caught very early in the morning while they are numb with cold. Their feet and wings are removed and the bodies roasted, broiled or stewed. When plentiful they are preserved in brine for future use. They caused havoc in the fields, stripping every vestige of green from trees, bushes and plants.

# SYCAMINE AND MUSTARD

One day Jesus was talking to His followers and they said: "Increase our faith."

Jesus looked at them. How could he show that however small our faith it could grow strong enough to do great deeds. He would tell them a story about things they knew well.

"If you had faith as small as a grain of mustard, you would be able to tell the great sycamine tree to be uprooted and to plant itself in the sea." (St. Luke 17.5-6.)

The sycamine has fruits rather like a long blackberry, but it is not one fruit, but many, each having had a separate flower. They grow so closely together that they appear as one. The heart-shaped leaves are rough and of a rich green.

The MUSTARD is a plant. In some lands it grows so tall that it is said a rider on horseback could be hidden in it! Generally it is nothing like so high. In England you can see fields of it, bright lemon in colour, a beautiful sight.

Its seeds are tiny and when ground into powder form mustard is used with various dishes to give flavour – a hot flavour! This powder may be made into poulices or plasters for certain illnesses. In some lands the leaves are eaten as a vegetable and are said to be healthful.

## THE ALMUG TREE

Don't confuse this with the ALGUM, which is a Grecian conifer.

The ALMUG provided sweet smelling wood for Solomon's Temple. It was also used for musical instruments such as the harp and psaltery. It is a native of India and is known as sandalwood. The wood is so antiseptic that no insects can live in it. The timber is heavy, black outside and red inside. It contains tannin which, when mixed with other ingredients, gives a good dye. The blossoms are pea-like. Sandalwood, in later times, was sprinkled on couches and about the room to give a pleasant smell. Almug is mentioned in 1. Kings. 10; 11.

Algum wood was also sent to King Solomon by Hiram, King of Tyre, 2. Chronicles. 2; 8.

# HIS FIRST MIRACLE

There was going to be a wedding at Cana of Galilee.

Everyone loves a wedding with its solemn rites and joyous festivities. Never does a girl look so radiant as on this day, whether she walks down the aisle in a European Church in her white gown, or in the more colourful Eastern costume, to make the vows after the manner of her people.

Cana was a tumbledown little place at the foot of bare hills. There was a mixture of stone houses and mudlike huts, a few grander places, olive gardens, dark cypresses and narrow streets busy with traffic.

It was only four miles from Nazareth. Had the bride and groom, as children, run in and out of the carpenter's shop? When older, had they talked of serious things with a beloved Friend? How pleased Mary would be as she watched the little gatherings, for Joseph was dead now and she was often alone.

It would be wonderful if He came to bless the wedding, thought the couple. Already He was becoming known as a Teacher . . . .

Today the tables in that peasant home groaned under the weight of good things: plump purple figs, nuts, citrus fruit, olives, meat, fish, herbs, cheese made from goats' milk and plenty of the rough sour local wine.

The bride and groom waited with their friends for Jesus. Then He arrived, with Mary His Mother and one or two of His followers. Everything was perfect, now. If there were any little awkward silences, Jesus would be ready with a merry quip...a ripple of laughter would run round the gathering.

The little bride smiled proudly; the groom's face glowed with pleasure. Jesus was here!

Mary must have been well known to that household, and as time passed and drinking vessels were filled and refilled, she saw an anxious look on the face of the master of ceremonies, who was an older relation of the groom.

He was glancing worriedly at the wine jars as the servants went to them again and again to pour out more drink for the guests.

Suppose the wine supply ran out? It *could* happen – but how dreadful that would be! The couple's memories would forever be tinged with regret. Angry words would pass, and blame would be fixed first on one side then on the other.

Mary looked at the happy little bride, whose myrtle wreath was a little aslant; at the master of ceremonies as he bit his lips – looking from the servants to the guests, to the wine jars . . . to the servants. Yes, the worst had happened!

She turned to Jesus. "They have no more wine," she whispered.

He looked at His mother and said gently, courteously,

"Dear lady, what is that to Me . . . to you? My time has not yet come."

She said no more, but smiled at Him, and then went to the servants and told them "Whatever He tells you to do, do it."

When they would have been voluble in their relief, she stilled their thanks and hurried to her place.

Then Jesus said to the servants: "Fill the pots with water."

Oh, their horrified looks! For one dreadful moment the men stared at the honoured Guest . . . "with *water*?"

You didn't drink water, much less offer it to a guest!

The thought was a flash only – a quick look at Mary – her nod – "Whatsoever He tells you to do, do it" – the authority in the command made them obey.

"Now pour it out and take it to the Master of Ceremonies," Jesus said. With many an inward tremor they obeyed. A rich ruby stream poured into the upheld vessels – murmurs of appreciation filled the room.

The Master of Ceremonies called the servant. "Why have you kept the best wine until the last?" he asked angrily. "You should have served it first, when people's taste is more discerning."

As the guests drank the new wine, unaware of the wonder, a hush fell upon the gathering.

The Master of Ceremonies sighed with relief. Mary looked at her Son. The little bride slipped her hand into that of her husband . . . and Jesus smiled at them.

We hear of the couple no more. Did they ever learn of this first Miracle? I think so – and the memory helped them through the bad times, rounded off the good days. Jesus had been at their wedding!

# CUSTOMS AND SAYINGS

## THE LOST COIN

In Bethlehem the women wore a sort of *helmet* headdress from which hung a chain of ten coins with a central medallion. It was the bridegroom's gift to the girl on marriage and was, naturally, greatly treasured. If she lost a part of it her husband might think she had been careless because she had little affection for it, or him.

This makes the 'Parable of the Lost Coin' clear. It was *more* than a mere coin which the woman had lost. What wonder that she told of her joy when it was found (Luke 15. 8. 9).

## SAYINGS

"Suffer me first to bury my father," (Matthew 8.21; Luke 9.59).

You would think that the speaker's father had just died. But in Oriental lands the saying was simply a procrastination – probably the man's father was hale and hearty, though getting on in years. The reply meant: "Wait until my father's dead and I'll think about it."

"Woman, what is that to you? My Hour is not yet come."

I expect you have wondered why Our Lord should appear to speak so rudely to His Mother, but we know that he was never rude, least of all to her. If you could read Greek you would find the line means something like this: "Lady, what is it to do with you or Me? It's not *My* wedding", but early translators thought it would be wrong for our Lord to jest. Yet often He *did* jest and if we could read the original manuscripts we might detect His jokes. Whatever the words, Mary knew what He meant, for she warned the servants to do *exactly* as her Son said.

## CUSTOMS

Friends walked hand in hand, never arm in arm.

The Palestinians would not sleep in a dark room as it was believed that a light kept away evil spirits.

Bread must not be cut; the loaves were of such a shape and pattern that they could be broken easily into pieces. Such a piece might be used as a spoon (opsarion) to be dipped into the common dish.

## BAR MITZVAH

When a Jewish boy reaches twelve years in Eastern and thirteen in Western countries he becomes a Son of Commandment: Bar-Mitzvah.

It is the most important day in his life. On the first Sabbath after the appointed age he is asked to read the lesson for the day in the synagogue, where he may also undergo a verbal examination, after which there is a reception at home and his presents are on view.

He is now considered a man and is qualified to form one of the ten men necessary for the holding of a Jewish service.

# SOME TITLES OF OUR LORD

Do you know these titles by which Our Lord was called?

1. And you shall call His Name . . . . .
2. And His name shall be called E . . . . . . .
3. Where is He who has been born K . . . of the . . . . ?
4. He shall be great and shall be called the S . . of the . . . . . . . .
5. He will be called Holy, the . . . of . . .
6. Prepare the way of the . . . .
7. The Ch . . . . of G . .
8. Good T . . . . . . (or R . . . .) what good thing shall I do to inherit eternal life?
9. And the W . . . became flesh and dwelt among us.
10. Behold the . . . . of God.

Titles used by Our Lord.

1. Jesus said to her "I am the R . . . . . . . . . . . and the Life."
2. I am the G . . . S . . . . . . .
3. I am the B . . . . of Life.
4. I am the L , . . . of the . . . . .
5. – of him will the . . . of . . . be ashamed.

Can you find other titles?

*Answers on page 126*

## DO YOU KNOW?

The eastern shepherd *leads* his flocks. They know his voice and follow and obey him as your dog obeys you. The sheep are more lively than English sheep and respond readily. One traveller notes that a shepherd actually made his sheep dance to his music! Often the owner's children or relations tended the flock, though wealthy owners would hire shepherds.

# THE STORM

It had been very hot that day and all Capurnaum seemed to have turned out to see the new teacher, Jesus, who was making the little fishing town His headquarters.

Through the long day there had been a steady stream of people asking the Master to heal them or their relatives; to comfort them or to bless their children.

"Surely some of them must just want to *listen*," thought one of the disciples. Jesus had so many plans for everyone, but they seemed too full of their own cares and little aches and pains.

"It must be very disappointing to Jesus," said John, "and He must be very weary working so hard always for others."

As the day passed and evening drew near, Jesus knew He must take a little rest, and He asked Peter to get out a boat. They would sail to the other side of the lake, away from the crowds, for a few hours of peace and quiet.

"And about time," muttered Peter as he crossed the sand to the boat.

Soon Jesus and His special friends were aboard, and almost at once the Master fell asleep in the stern, as the others rowed on the still water.

But it seemed as if they weren't to get away so easily, for anyone who had a boat, or could beg a place on one, was following.

But storms rose suddenly on the Sea of Galilee, as people called the lake deep in the Jordan valley. The wind rose and raced through the gorge as through a funnel, tossing the boats about as if they were made of paper, and now the sky became overcast, with all the signs of an oncoming storm, and the small boats returned to shore, leaving just the one to sail on for the seven miles in the teeth of the gale.

The storm gathered force; great waves threatened to overturn the boat, and still Jesus slept. Now the wind raged fiercely, howling as the water crashed in mountainous sheets and, fishermen though they were and used to the sea, the disciples began to wonder if they would ever reach the other side.

As the men lurched, clinging together in fear, they felt they could bear the terror no longer. Didn't their Master care that they were likely to be flung overboard any moment? How could He sleep when the spray was drenching Him? How could He sleep through the din and terror of this raging storm? Wouldn't He mind if His friends were drowned?

"I'm going to waken Him," decided Peter. he struggled across the swaying deck. Even if he were washed into the sea, anything was better than facing the storm alone.

"Master, Master," he yelled above the clamour, "waken. Don't you care if we drown?"

Jesus stirred, stood up and walked to the side of the boat, looking at the angry seas. Then he said, quietly, "Be calm, now. Be still . . ."

The men stared.

The wind died away, the huge waves settled quietly and gently and the leaden skies were deeply blue, flecked with a host of stars.

Jesus smiled, and turned to the men.

"Wasn't your faith great enough to know you would be safe with Me?" He asked.

Then, peacefully, they sailed to the other side of the lake.

# THE SMALL BOY
# AND THE MIRACLE

Jonas stood there, impatiently, as his mother tied some barley loaves – which were rather like bread cakes – and a few pickled fish, into a piece of rough linen.

"And be sure you bring my cloth back," she said as she kissed him and sent him on his way.

Soon he came to the fields and found a small stream, but it was only a trickle, so he collected some stones and built a dam, but even then it was so small that he could only dabble his toes in the rather muddy water, so he sat back, broke a bread cake, stuffed it with fish and ate it slowly, to make it last longer.

Presently he grew tired of his own company. He would go to the lakeside. The fishermen might be there mending their nets and they always had plenty of stories to tell.

He raced along, jumping over boulders, chasing butterflies, but as it grew hotter he slowed down, until he came to a dip in the fields, and he stood staring upwards – for there, on the hillside, were crowds and crowds of people. But what were they doing there? He'd just have to go and see for himself.

When he reached the fringe of the crowd he couldn't see anything, so he pushed and shoved, sometimes getting a slap as he trod on someone's toes, until he stood on a little grassy place at the front where there was a small group of people. One Man was talking. It was Jesus!

Jonas sat down, prepared to eat and listen, but he soon forgot all about food.

The Teacher was talking about the Kingdom of Heaven. It seemed a very nice place, thought the lad, but to get there you must be good, kind to your neighbours – and sometimes your neighbours weren't the sort of people you *wanted* to be kind to. Now Jesus was telling a story.

"The Kingdom of Heaven is like a wonderful pearl – so wonderful that a man who wanted it sold everything he had in order to buy it."

Through the heat of the day Jonas sat there entranced.

Presently Jesus spoke to the group of men by His side. He was saying that the crowd must be hungry and must be fed.

One of the men laughed and said there were no shops there and even if there were they hadn't enough money to buy bread for all that throng.

Andrew, one of the men, looked at Jonas and his open bundle, and turned to Jesus and said, feeling a little foolish: "There's a boy here with – er – five barley loaves and two small fish – but they aren't enough for so many . . ."

There was a burst of laughter – but Jesus didn't laugh.

Jonas jumped up. If the Master wanted his picnic meal He should have it.

Jesus took the bundle and smiled at the lad. Then He spoke quietly, but Jonas heard quite plainly. He was asking for a blessing on the food, and then He took the bread and broke it and gave it to His friends and told them to give it to the people – and the fish as well . . . and He kept breaking the bread and giving it; breaking it, giving it – and there was enough for all.

Enough for a boy's picnic; enough fo. thousands. More than enough, for some began to throw bits away. Jesus didn't like that. He told his friends to try to find some baskets, nothing must be wasted.

And there were twelve baskets full of the pieces.

Jonas's eyes were round with wonder. He had actually helped with a Miracle!

# PLEASE

God made the lovely countryside,
He made the flowers to open wide;
To close at night or in the rain
And then to open wide again.

God made the seaside in His way,
A pleasant place for holiday;
Though people change it to *their* style
With noise and bustle all the while.

God made the sands where children play,
The waves to take great ships away;
The sun by day, the moon by night,
To give the world its share of light.

God made us know what's right, what's wrong;
To mourn, to weep, to sing a song;
Yet some delight to spoil and break
The lovely things His people make.

They do not feel a proper pride
In caring for the countryside;
In tending gardens in the town
Where little plots of flowers are grown.

It is a pity just to spoil
Things made by God or wrought by toil;
So, when you see a bird or flower,
*Please* do not shorten its brief hour.

# THE SMALL MAN

**(Read St. Luke 19.1–9)**

Zacchaeus was a publican.

In the days of Jesus, publicans were those who paid the foreign rulers a lump sum of money and collected it back from the people in taxes. No one likes to pay taxes, but when these were charged at unjust, high rates, the tax collectors were hated and despised.

Zacchaeus was a small man. When a crowd gathered he was pushed and jostled – often on purpose – what could he do when folk apologised profusely? So though Zacchaeus might start at the front of a crowd when some fine procession was in progress, he always ended up at the back. Even if he stood on tiptoe and craned his neck, he might just as well have stayed at home for he didn't get as much as a glimpse of the cause of the commotion and, worse, he might be hurt or have his cloak torn in the process.

One day, as he sat in his office in Jericho, he heard the news – Jesus was coming that way! Everyone was talking about it! Zacchaeus had heard a lot about the great Teacher and Prophet. Here was a chance to *see* Him. He put away his scrolls and money bags, locked his office and set out.

*This* time he *would* see Jesus, whatever happened.

He made his way past flower-filled gardens, past trees covered with blossom, and joined the crowd of people who were hurrying to the main road, talking excitedly.

But there were so many people! Already the small man was being pushed about, but he was determined to catch a glimpse of Jesus, if no more than a glimpse. But how? The main road was growing more and more crowded with men, women and children. Zacchaeus looked about. It was hopeless. It was like standing behind a wall of people, each jostling for a better position.

Nearby grew an old, gnarled sycamore tree. In season it would be full of clusters of fig-mulberries; now it was leafy and the branches were almost asking to be climbed.

"Can I do it?" he chuckled to himself, feeling more a mischievous schoolboy than a staid, successful business man.

He tied his cloak about himself, put a foot on a lower and a hand on a higher branch, and managed to pull himself up until he had a marvellous view of the road.

This was splendid!

He perched there, well satisfied, a broad smile on his face at having found a way to see Jesus without any crushing or pushing.

There was a hustle and bustle among the crowd below. It could mean only one thing: Jesus was coming into view! Yes, there He was in the distance accompanied by a small group. They would be His followers, thought Zacchaeus Six? Seven? A dozen? It didn't matter – why waste time counting them when the people below were surging forward, shouting, yelling, singing.

*They* hadn't such a good view! Zacchaeus felt quite proud of the way he'd overcome his usual disappointments.

"It's to be hoped this bough doesn't break," he thought, but with good humour.

Then he forgot his precarious position, for the Teacher was coming nearer. Zacchaeus could see His kindly, forceful face as He glanced from side to side, stopping now and then to talk to sinners – Zacchaeus remembered that it was said He'd always time for such folk – or to touch a child in blessing, until at last He was very near the sycamore tree.

"Well, I've seen everything now," said the small man to himself happily.

Jesus stopped and looked right up into the tree with a smile that broadened in amusement.

"Zacchaeus," He called, "hurry up and come down, for I will stay at your house today."

The little man almost fell from his perch with surprise.

He scrambled down as fast as he could, not caring if the branches scratched him, so long as he could be near Jesus.

"Stay with me?" he whispered incredulously. "Oh, Master, how glad I shall be to welcome you."

As he stood humbly there, those near began to grumble and mutter, turning to stare at the publican.

No respectable Jew would dine with a – a – *publican.* Weren't they hand in glove with the hated Roman conquerors? Didn't they squeeze the money out of the poor to grow fat and wealthy?

They hurled the questions at Jesus. Zacchaeus stood speechless.

Then at last he found his tongue.

"Oh, Lord," he said humbly, "I will give half my money to the poor and if I have wronged anyone I will give it back to him fourfold."

Jesus looked at him.

Then he spoke gently: "This day salvation has come to your house."

This was the most wonderful day he had ever known, thought the small man, as he hurried home to make ready for Jesus.

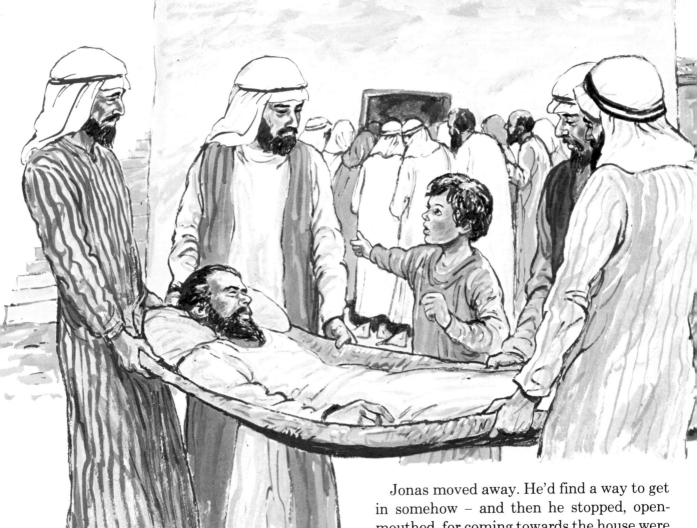

# THE PARALYZED MAN

(From a boy's point of view. Who can say there weren't any children about at the time? I have called him Jonas. Read St. Mark 2.1-12.)

Jonas walked along the street of Capernaum kicking a stone along with his sandalled foot.

Suddenly he noticed a crowd of people outside a house. Crowds always meant something exciting, so he ran quickly and tried to push his way through, asking breathlessly: "What's the matter? What's happened?"

"The Teacher Jesus is inside talking," said a man, "and by the looks of it, everyone else has pushed in, too. It's no place for lads . . . be off . . . be off . . . ."

Jonas moved away. He'd find a way to get in somehow – and then he stopped, open-mouthed, for coming towards the house were four men, carrying a sleeping mat, like a stretcher. On it lay a pale-faced man – the paralyzed man who couldn't even move.

"You'll not get in," said Jonas. "I'm not big, and I can't squeeze through *that* crush."

The sick man sighed hopelessly, but his friends weren't so easily discouraged. If they could get him to the roof top they could lower him down to the courtyard – surely Jesus would take pity on him?

It was a good idea. The men told their friend and then hurried to a boat on the shore and came back with some lengths of rope.

They tied a piece to each end of the sleeping mat and with difficulty climbed the outside steps. Jonas crept after them but they were too intent on their task to notice.

Then the boy heard cries of disappointment; instead of being open to the sky, the house was lightly covered with sun-baked mud tiles!

The four men wouldn't be beaten, though. They clawed at the tiles until they had made a hole big enough for their purpose. Then they gently lowered the sick man down, ignoring the angry shouts of the people below, who scurried aside out of danger.

The mat moved dizzily and then settled right at the feet of Jesus, who watched with comical appreciation this impudent, but kindly trick.

The paralyzed man lay there, fearful of the anger of the crowd and, perhaps, of Jesus. But the Master was looking at him with understanding and compassion.

"Cheer up, My son," he said gently, "cheer up. Your sins are forgiven."

There was a gasp from the men on the roof. They hadn't brought him to have his sins forgiven but to have his paralysis cured. The crowd muttered angrily. Who was this Man to say: "Your sins are forgiven" when only the Lord God had power to forgive sins? He was just showing off, pretending to be as great as God.

Jesus looked at the furious people.

"Which is easier," He asked, "to say 'Your sins are forgiven' or to say 'Get up and walk'?"

The crowd stared uneasily, without answering, as Jesus spoke to the sick man. "Get up, My son. Roll up your mat and walk."

Breathlessly the crowd waited.

It couldn't happen . . . of course it couldn't . . . but they waited . . . .

As if new life had come to him, the paralyzed man stood up . . . picked up his mat and rolled it under his arm, and – I'm sure with a grateful look at Jesus – walked out, the silent crowd making way for him.

The four on the roof looked at each other, and then joined in the outburst of praise and thanksgiving before hurrying down the steps to meet their joyful friend.

# ANSWERS

## OLD TESTAMENT

Page 10

### Birds of the Bible

1. Pelican; 2. Owl; 3. Peacock; 4. a and b. Swan; 5. Pigeon (rock dove); 6. Griffon vulture.

Page 18

### Family Tree Quiz

Isaac (father and grandson); Rebekah (brother); Leah and Rachel.

Page 21

### Quick Quiz

1. Oats; 2. Potatoes; 3. Rice.

Page 29

### Places Quiz

1. Mount Ararat; 2. Euphrates; 3. Canaan; 4. Egypt; 5. On; 6. Heliopolis; 7. Beer-sheba.

### Find the Stranger

1. c. Zion (Jerusalem); the others are sisters. 2. b. a. country; the others are rivers. 3.a. a ruler; the others are brothers. 4.a. a place; the others are brothers. 5.c. a weed; the others are musical instruments. 6.c. a bag; the others are 'trumpets' (the shofar is the ram's horn).

Page 44

### Right or Wrong?

1. Wrong, with the Creation; 2. Wrong, 11; 3. Right; 4. Wrong, Reuben and Judah objected; 5. Right; 6. Wrong, Egypt; 7. Right; 8. Wrong; 9. Right; 10. Wrong; 11. Wrong; 12. Right.

### Jumbled Fruits

1. Apple (Apricot); 2. Blackberry; 3. Cucumber; 4. Melon.

Page 52

### Right or Wrong

1. Wrong; 2. Right; 3. Wrong, at Shiloh; 4. Right; 5. Right; 6. Wrong. He said, "The God of Israel answer your petition." He did not know for what she prayed; 7. Right; 8. Wrong, she came annually; 9. Right; 10. Wrong, four times; 11. Wrong; 12. Wrong. Thy Servant hears.

1. Speak, for thy servant hears.
2. And the child Samuel ministered unto the Lord.
3. And Eli perceived that the Lord had called the child.
4. My heart exults in the Lord, my strength is exalted in the Lord.
5. And Samuel grew and the Lord was with him and let none of his words fall to the ground.

## NEW TESTAMENT

Page 70

### Missing Words

1. Birds (St. Matthew 6.26); 2. lilies (St. Matthew 6.28); 3. hen; chickens (St. Matthew 23.37) or brood R.S.V.); 4. dove (St. Luke 3.22); 5. sparrows (St. Matthew 10.29).

Page 78

### A Bible Quiz

1. Right; 2. Right; 3. Wrong. They were the first to hear; 4. Wrong. No one knows if they took gifts, but many Nativity Plays introduce such offerings; 5. Right; 6. Magi is a Persian word meaning wise men or astrologers. The term "wise men" appears in St. Matthew's Gospel (2.1); 7. Wrong. They found Him in a house. (St. Matthew 2.11); 8. Wrong. Persian gods, said to be Ahura-Mazda, the god of light; 9. Right. (St. Matthew 2. 1–3 but read to verse 12); 10. Wrong. Herod intended to kill the Child (St. Matthew 2.13); 11. Wrong (St. Matthew 2.13); 12. The coming of the Wise Men, known as the Manifestation of Christ to the Gentiles. Gentiles are people who are not Jews.

Page 91

### Map Quiz

1. Jerusalem; Jericho (St. Luke 10.30); 2. Cana (St. John 2. 1–11. The story is retold for you on pages 51.53); 3. Bethlehem (St. Luke 2.15–16); 4. Galilee; 5. Mediterranean; 6. Jordan; 7. Jerusalem; 8. Temple; 9. Nazareth (St. Luke 26.27); 10. Capernaum (St. Luke 4.31); 11. Bethany (St. John 12.1); 12. City; Jerusalem.

Page 96

### Who?

1. Angel Gabriel to the Virgin Mary. (St. Luke 1.28); 2. The Virgin Mary to the Angel (St. Luke 1.38); 3. Angels to the shepherds (St. Luke 2.13.14); 4. Simeon, the priest, to God (St. Luke 2.29); 5. Jesus to His audience, (St. Luke 20.25. Read from verse 19); 6. The Devil, to Jesus in the Wilderness (St. Luke 4.3); 7. Jesus to His disciples and the crowd. Sermon on the Mount (St. Matthew 7.1); 8. Pilate to the Jews who brought Jesus to Trial (St. John 18.38); 9. Jesus as He was nailed on the Cross to God (St. Luke 23.34); 10. Jesus to His Mother and St. John (St. John 19.26.27); 11. Mary Magdalene to the two Angels after the Resurrection (St. John 20.13); 12. Jesus to His Apostles in the Upper Room on the evening of the Day of Resurrection (St John 20.22, 23).

Page 116

### Some Titles of Our Lord

1. Jesus (St. Luke 1.31); 2. Emmanuel (St. Matthew 1.23); 3. King of the Jews (St. Matthew 2.2); 4. Son of the Most High (St. Luke 1.32); 5. Son of God (St. Luke 1.35); 6. Lord (St. Luke 3.4); 7. Christ of God (St. Luke 9.20); 8. Teacher. Rabbi (So many references it is suggested that you find one or two for yourself). 9. Word (St. John 1.1); 10. Lamb (St. John 1.29).

### Titles used by Our Lord

1. Resurrection (St. John 11.25); 2. Good Shepherd (St. John 10.11); 3. Bread (St. John 6.35); 4. Light of the world (St. John 8.12); 5. Son of Man (St. Luke 9–22).

Remember that there are several different versions of the Bible. The one generally used is called the AUTHORISED VERSION (R.V.) Then there is the REVISED STANDARD VERSION (R.S.V.) The Jerusalem Bible, the New English Bible. I have used all of these with the exception of the last named. Some of my quotations may not be *quite* the same as your Bible, as some versions use more modern words. Can you find out several different renderings of a quotation?